HANDBOOK OF WWII GERMAN MILITARY SYMBOLS AND ABBREVIATIONS 1943–45

Terrence Booth

HELION & COMPANY

Helion and Company
26 Willow Road
Solihull
West Midlands
B91 1UE
England
Tel. 0121 705 3393
Fax 0121 711 4075
Email: publishing@helion.co.uk
Website: http://www.helion.co.uk

Published by Helion and Company, 2001
Designed and typeset by Bookcraft Ltd, Stroud, Gloucestershire
Printed by The Cromwell Press, Trowbridge, Wiltshire

© Helion and Company 2001

ISBN 1 874622 85 X

British Library Cataloguing-in-Publication Data.
A catalogue record for this book is available from the British Library.

For details of other military history titles published by Helion and Company
contact the above address, or visit our website: http://www.helion.co.uk.

We always welcome receiving book proposals from prospective authors, particu-
larly those relating to the Second World War German Armed Forces.

Contents

Introduction

This book aims to provide the reader with a clear and comprehensive reference to the symbols and signs seen in photos, tables of organisation and maps for the period 23 May 1943 onwards. It should be noted that the symbols seen in this book replaced an earlier set in use up until 23 May 1943, and it was still common practise for some of the earlier symbols to be found in the field during the 1943–45 period, especially on vehicles.

I have found the experience of locating and drawing together the original documentation for this reference book both a challenge and a joy, and would like to give special thanks to Steven Walton from the Imperial War museum; Duncan Rogers from Helion and Company; Julianne Booth, my wife; and William McManus, for the support, knowledge, and time they contributed in the development of this book.

I welcome the reader's constructive input – should anyone have more founded information that would add to or correct any data, then I look forward to receiving this, so that future editions can include the corrections and additions necessary to ensure the authenticity and usefulness of this reference. All correspondence should be directed care of the publishers, whose contact details can be found on the reverse of the title page.

The first two parts of the book feature an overview of how the German Armed Forces used the symbols in the field. This includes a brief reference to the hierarchical organisation of the symbols that reflects the structure of the military at that time.

Parts III, IV and V of this book deal with specific forms/categories of symbols used by the German Armed Forces.

The format used throughout parts I to V has been to provide an image of the symbol, accompanied by the relevant German term and its English translation, along with any pertinent information that will aid the reader's understanding of the symbol and the unit that it represented.

The final part of the book, containing an extensive list of abbreviations and their German terms, supplemented by English translations, should prove invaluable to any reader who has more than a passing interest in the Second World War German Armed Forces.

Terrence Booth
March 2001

Publisher's Note

The publishers would like to express their thanks to David Westwood for his invaluable assistance during the preparation of this book.

PART I

BASICS: STRUCTURE OF THE SYMBOLS

The tactical symbols used by the Wehrmacht consisted of the basic tactical symbol together with additional symbols, letters and numbers.

BASIC TACTICAL SYMBOLS OF COMMANDS, HEADQUARTERS AND LEADERS OF UNITS

Army High Command		*Oberkommando des Heeres*
Army Group Command		*Heeresgruppenkommando*
Army Command		*Armeeoberkommando*
Military Commander of an area under Military Occupation		*Militärbefehlshaber*
Corps Command		*Generalkommando*
Divisional Command		*Divisionskommando*
Brigade HQ		*Brigadestab*
Regimental HQ		*Regimentsstab*

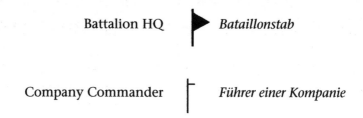

Battalion HQ   *Bataillonstab*

Company Commander   *Führer einer Kompanie*

The arm-of-service is shown by the addition of the basic arm-of-service symbol under, over, or besides the flagpole. Examples:

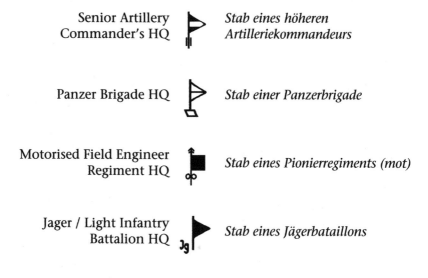

Senior Artillery Commander's HQ   *Stab eines höheren Artilleriekommandeurs*

Panzer Brigade HQ   *Stab einer Panzerbrigade*

Motorised Field Engineer Regiment HQ   *Stab eines Pionierregiments (mot)*

Jager / Light Infantry Battalion HQ   *Stab eines Jägerbataillons*

BASIC ARM-OF-SERVICE SYMBOLS

Infantry *Infanterie*

Mountain Troops *Gebirgstruppen*

Bicycle Units *Radfahreinheiten*

Motorcycle Infantry *Kraftradschützen*

Tank *Panzer*

Anti-Tank *Panzerjäger*

Cavalry *Kavallerie*

Artillery *Artillerie*

Anti-Aircraft Units and
Anti-Aircraft Artillery *Flakeinheiten und Flakartillerie*

Survey and Mapping Troops *Vermessungs- und Kartentruppen*

Field Engineers *Pioniere*

Fortress Engineers *Festungspioniere*

Construction Engineers *Baupioniertruppen*

Rocket Launcher / Nebelwerfer Troops	人	*Nebeltruppen*
Signals and Communication Troops	↑ oder ⬡	*Nachrichtentruppen*
Railway Troops	⬆	*Eisenbahntruppen*
Field Railway Units	●	*Feldeisenbahneinheiten*
Inland Waterway Survey Troops	⛴	*Feldwasserstraßeneinheiten*
Technical Troops	T	*Technische Truppen*
Propaganda Troops	Ͱ	*Propagandatruppen*
Supply Troops	⚲ oder ⚲	*Nachschubtruppen*
Medical Troops	✛	*Sanitätstruppen*
Veterinarian Troops	⚕	*Veterinärtruppen*
Ordnance Troops	✕	*Feldzeugtruppen*
Motor Transport Park Troops	✳	*Kraftfahrparktruppen*
Water Supply Troops	W	*Wasserversorgungstruppen*
Military Police	⚲	*Feldgendarmerie*

WWII GERMAN MILITARY SYMBOLS

Army Post Office   ⌣⌣   *Feldpost*

Rear-Area Care Units   ◗   *Betreuungseinheiten*

Patrol Services   ◆   *Streifendienste*

Platoon-sized units are generally represented by the basic infantry symbol with the addition of the corresponding arm-of-service symbol in, over or besides it. Examples:

Platoon of a Mountain Infantry Company	☐ + ▲ = ☐		*Zug einer Gebirgsjägerkompanie*
Platoon of a Field Engineer Company	☐ + ↑ = ☐		*Zug einer Pionierkompanie*
Platoon of a Regional Defence Company	☐ + Ls = Ls☐		*Zug einer Landesschützenkompanie*

To represent a company, the left-hand side of the symbol is thickened. Example:

Construction Engineer Company   ☒ + | = ☒   *Baupionierkompanie*

Infantry Gun, Bicycle, Motorcycle, Panzer, Anti-tank and Armoured car platoons are represented by the basic arm-of-service symbol. Examples:

Platoon of an Infantry Gun Company   ⊥   *Zug einer I. G. Kompanie*

Platoon of a Panzer Company   ▱   *Zug einer Panzerkompanie*

For these arms-of-service, a company is represented by a thickened line. Examples:

Anti-Tank Company	T + | = T	*Panzerjägerkompanie*
Armoured Car Company	⌐◯ + | = ⌐◯	*Panzerspähkompanie*
Company of Motorcycle Infantry	⊗ + O = ⊗	*Kraftradschützen-kompanie*

Symbols for Artillery and Nebelwerfer platoons and batteries give the number of guns or rocket launchers as a figure, underneath the weapon symbol. Example:

| Light Howitzer Battery of 4 guns | /e \|4 | *leichte Haubitzbatterie zu 4 Geschützen* |

BASIC WEAPON SYMBOLS

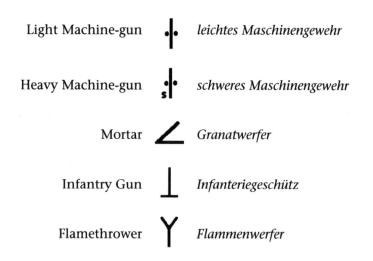

Light Machine-gun	•|•	*leichtes Maschinengewehr*
Heavy Machine-gun	s•|•	*schweres Maschinengewehr*
Mortar	∠	*Granatwerfer*
Infantry Gun	⊥	*Infanteriegeschütz*
Flamethrower	Y	*Flammenwerfer*

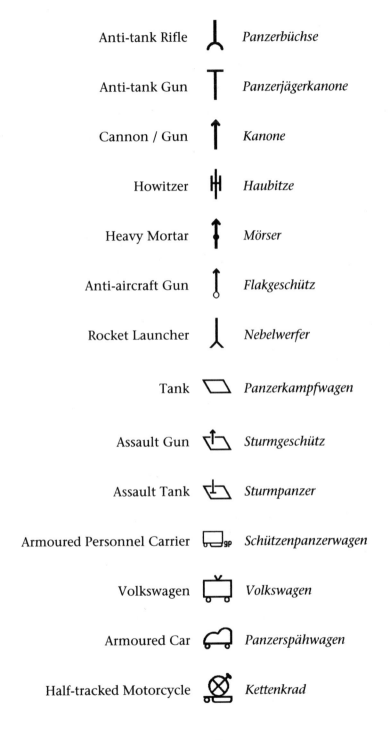

Anti-tank Rifle		*Panzerbüchse*
Anti-tank Gun		*Panzerjägerkanone*
Cannon / Gun		*Kanone*
Howitzer		*Haubitze*
Heavy Mortar		*Mörser*
Anti-aircraft Gun		*Flakgeschütz*
Rocket Launcher		*Nebelwerfer*
Tank		*Panzerkampfwagen*
Assault Gun		*Sturmgeschütz*
Assault Tank		*Sturmpanzer*
Armoured Personnel Carrier		*Schützenpanzerwagen*
Volkswagen		*Volkswagen*
Armoured Car		*Panzerspähwagen*
Half-tracked Motorcycle		*Kettenkrad*

For detailed identification of the weapon, numbers and letters are added to the symbol in the following manner:

- the calibre of the weapon is placed to the left of the symbol
- the range of the weapon is placed above the symbol
- the origin of the weapon is placed to the right of the symbol
- the number of pieces to which the symbol applies is placed below the symbol

Example:

10.5 cm Light Field
Howitzer Battery,
Range 11km,
of Belgian manufacture,
with 3 guns

10,5cm le F. H. Batterie
Schutzweite 11km
belgischer Herkunft zu 3
Geschützen

Arms of the same type but varying calibre within a unit are shown one after another, under the symbol, connected with a '+' sign. The information is read from left to right starting with the largest calibre. Example:

| 2 Heavy and 6 Light Infantry Guns | 2 + 6 | *2 schwere und 6 leichte Infanteriegeschütze* |
| 3 Heavy and 6 Light Mortars | 3 + 0 + 6 | *3 schwere und 6 leichte Granatwerfer* |

Weapons of the same calibre, but of varying tube lengths have the following letters placed to the right of the calibre, or to the right of the number of pieces/vehicles or vehicle mark:

- k = short
- l = long

Examples:

2 Mortars, 8cm Calibre with Long Barrel	8ℓ ⟋ **2**	*2 Granatwerfer, Kaliber 8cm mit langem Rohr*
Medium Panzer Company of 10 Panzer IV's with Long-barreled Guns and 3 Panzer IV's with Short-barreled Guns	⬭ m 10/Ⅳℓ+3/ⅣK	*Mittlere Panzerkompanie zu 10 Panzer IV langes Rohr und 3 Panzer IV kurzes Rohr*

To further categorise weapons, additional letters are used. These are *l, m, s* or *sw*. These are placed to the left-hand side of the symbols.

	人	⊥	∠	T	人
Light *leicht (le)*	up to 7.9 mm	up to 7.5 cm	up to 7.9 cm	up to 3.9 cm	up to 10.9 cm
Medium *mittel (m)*			8–11.9 cm	4–5.9 cm	11–15.9 cm
Heavy *schwer (s)*	from 8 mm	from 7.6 cm	from 12 cm	6–8.9 cm	16–21.9 cm
Super-Heavy *schwerste (sw)*				from 9 cm	from 22 cm

	↑	⊬	↑	⥮
Light *leicht (le)*	up to 9.9 cm	12.9 cm		up to 3.6 cm
Medium *mittel (m)*				3.7–5.9 cm
Heavy *schwer (s)*	10–20.9 cm	13–20.9 cm	21–24.9 cm	6–15.9 cm
Super-Heavy *schwerste (sw)*	from 21 cm	from 21 cm	from 25 cm	from 16 cm

Example:

Motorised Infantry Company with 6 Heavy Machine-guns 12 Light Machine-guns 1 Heavy Anti-tank Rifle 3 Light Anti-tank Rifles 3 Light Mortars	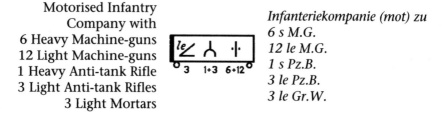	*Infanteriekompanie (mot) zu* *6 s M.G.* *12 le M.G.* *1 s Pz.B.* *3 le Pz.B.* *3 le Gr.W.*

As with the weapon symbols, vehicles have additional letters or numbers added to their basic symbol. Example:

Panzer III 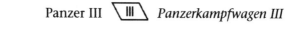 *Panzerkampfwagen III*

Light Armoured Personnel Carrier   *leichter Schützenpanzerwagen*

The same applies to units. Example:

Medium Panzer Company   ◢m◣   *Mittlere Panzerkompanie*

BASIC SYMBOLS USED TO DENOTE MEANS OF MOBILITY

Units using wheeled motor vehicles have the following symbol added to their basic symbol: o   o

Examples:

Motorised Infantry   *Stab eines Infanteriebataillons*
Battalion HQ   *(mot)*

Motorised Infantry Company   *Infanteriekompanie (mot)*

Part-motorised units are designated by the following: o

Examples:

HQ of a Part-Motorised *Stab eines*
Mountain Engineer Battalion   *Gebirgspionierbataillons (tmot)*

Part-Motorised Signals *Nachrichtenkompanie (tmot)*
Company of an Infantry   *einer Infanteriedivision*
Division

Units made part-mobile through the use of horses and motor vehicles are denoted by the following symbol: ⌐⌐

Example:

HQ of a Part-Mobile
Anti-tank Battalion

Stab einer Panzerjägerabteilung
(t bew.)

Units made part-mobile through the use of motor vehicles are given the following symbol: ⌐⌐⌐

HQ of a Part-Mobile
Artillery Battalion

Stab einer Artillerieabteilung
(t bew. mot)

Units utilising prime movers (e.g. trucks) are denoted by the following symbol: σ—σ

Units utilizing the *Raupenschlepper Ost* (a tracked prime-mover) are designated by the letters "RSO" placed next to the mobility symbol.

Examples:

Battery of Rocket Launchers
with Prime-mover-tows

Batterie Nebelwerfer (mot Z)

Battery of Light Field
Howitzers with RSO-tows

Batterie le Feldhaubitze
(mot Z)

Units with fully-tracked vehicles are given the following symbol: ⊂⊃
Panzer units were, however, designated by a rhomboid symbol.

Examples:

Self-Propelled Anti-Tank
Gun Company   *Panzerjägerkompanie (Sf)*

Panzer Company   *Panzerkompanie*

Units with half-tracks are shown by the following: ☐

Example:

Armoured Reconnaissance
Company with Half-tracks   *Panzerspähkompanie mit
halbkette*

Units with amphibious vehicles are given the following: ✶

Example:

Amphibious Volkswagen   *Volksschwimmwagen*

The means of mobility of individual weapons is displayed by using the
same symbols as those used by units, as shown above. The same applies to
symbols used to represent winter-mobility (see below). The symbol illustrating the means of mobility is placed above or below the weapon
symbol. Examples:

Anti-tank Gun with
Prime-mover-tow   *Panzerjägerkanone,
durch Zg Kw fortbewegl.*

Anti-tank Gun
with Truck-tow
Panzerjägerkanone,
durch Lkw fortbewegl.

Horse-drawn weapons do not receive any additional symbol. Example:

Horse-drawn Heavy
Infantry Gun **S**
schweres Infanteriegeschütz
mit Pferden bespannt

When a weapon is stationery, or has no means of mobility, it is shown by
the following symbol: **X**

Example:

Unlimbered / Deployed
Anti-tank Gun
Panzerjägerkannone,
unbespannt

Winter-mobile units are indicated by the following:

Examples:

Jager / Light Infantry
Battalion, Winter-mobile **Jg** *Jägerbataillon, winterbeweglich*

Jager / Light Infantry
Company, Winter-mobile **Jg** *Jägerkompanie, winterbeweglich*

Anti-tank Company,
Winter-mobile
Panzerjägerkompanie,
winterbeweglich

Vehicles with sledge supports receive the winter-mobile symbol (as above) appended to their unit's tactical sign, with an 'Ah' added, as follows:

Panzer Company with 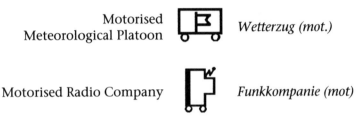 *Panzerkompanie mit*
Sledge Supports *Schlittenanhänger*

ADDITIONAL SYMBOLS

Additional symbols expand upon the membership or deployment of a unit. The meanings of these symbols are explained in the later sections of this book. In general, the additional symbol is situated, with few exceptions, on the flagpole or within the unit symbol. Examples:

Motorised *Wetterzug (mot.)*
Meteorological Platoon

Motorised Radio Company *Funkkompanie (mot)*

The addition of the following symbol to the tactical symbol signifies that the unit's role is predominantly that of reconnaissance:

Examples:

Panzer Reconnaissance *Stab einer*
Battalion HQ *Panzeraufklärungsabteilung*

Bicycle Reconnaissance *Radfahraufklärungsschwadron*
Squadron

The addition of the following symbol to the tactical symbol has a variety of meanings, dependent upon its position:

Examples:

Gun Battery in Position *Kanonenbatterie in Stellung*

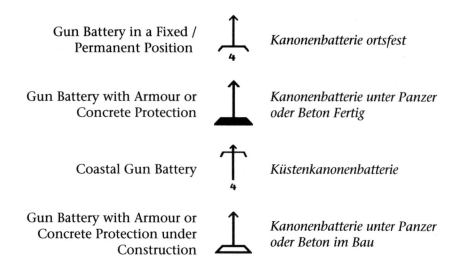

Gun Battery in a Fixed / Permanent Position — *Kanonenbatterie ortsfest*

Gun Battery with Armour or Concrete Protection — *Kanonenbatterie unter Panzer oder Beton Fertig*

Coastal Gun Battery — *Küstenkanonenbatterie*

Gun Battery with Armour or Concrete Protection under Construction — *Kanonenbatterie unter Panzer oder Beton im Bau*

ADDITIONAL LETTERS

The addition of the letters 'F, Gr, Jg, Ls, Sich, Str' indicates a special purpose, and these are placed to the left of the tactical symbol. Examples:

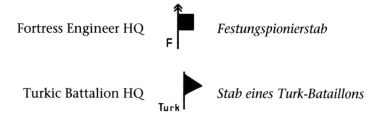

Fortress Engineer HQ — *Festungspionierstab*

Turkic Battalion HQ — *Stab eines Turk-Bataillons*

The additional letters representing the affiliation of staff and units are placed to the right of the tactical symbol, thus:

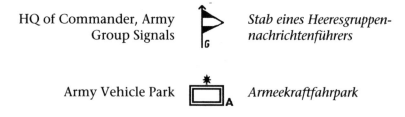

HQ of Commander, Army Group Signals — *Stab eines Heeresgruppen-nachrichtenführers*

Army Vehicle Park — *Armeekraftfahrpark*

The part of the Wehrmacht to which the unit belongs is denoted by the following letters:

Army	**H**	*Heer*
Navy	**M**	*Marine*
Air Force	**L**	*Luftwaffe*

These are placed besides the unit's number, or they might be denoted by the colour of the tactical symbol:

Black	*Heer*
Blue	*Marine*
Green	*Luftwaffe*

The origin of weapons or units is represented by additional letters placed to the right of the tactical symbol, as follows:

American	**a**	*amerikanisch*
Belgian	**b**	*belgisch*
Danish	**d**	*dänisch*
British	**e**	*englisch*
French	**f**	*französisch*
Greek	**g**	*griechisch*
Dutch	**h**	*holländisch*
Yugoslavian	**j**	*jugoslawisch*
Norwegian	**n**	*norwegisch*
Austrian	**ö**	*österreichisch*
Polish	**p**	*polnisch*
Russian	**r**	*russisch*
Czech	**t**	*tschechisch*

Example:

Heavy Self-Propelled Gun Battery 2./109, with equipment of French origin		*schwere Kanonenbatterie (Sf) 2./109 französischer herkunft*

The remaining additional letters denote the unit's special type or purpose. The letters are placed in, over, under or besides the tactical symbol.

Examples:

Motorised Decontamination Battery		*Entgiftungsbatterie (mot)*
Motorised Bridging Column with Type 'B' equipment (single road, 4½–20 ton capacity)		*Brückenkolonne (mot) B-Gerät*
Bus Column		*Kraftomnibuskolonne*
Large Bakery Company		*Großbäckereikompanie*

These letters are only valid when used in conjunction with the tactical symbol.

ADDITIONAL NUMBERS

Arabic numerals are added to the right, above or besides the tactical symbol to denote the staff or unit's number. Examples:

3rd Panzer Brigade HQ		*Stab der 3. Panzerbrigade*

5th Company,
1st Grenadier Regiment

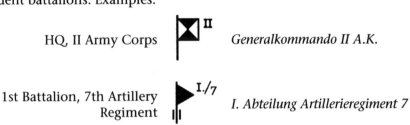

5/1

*5. Kompanie,
Grenadierregiment 1*

Roman numerals are used in a similar way, to denote corps and non-independent battalions. Examples:

HQ, II Army Corps

II

Generalkommando II A.K.

1st Battalion, 7th Artillery
Regiment

I./7

I. Abteilung Artillerieregiment 7

Weaponry symbols and numbers denote the unit's armament. Example:

Bicycle Reconnaissance
Squadron with
4 Heavy Machine-guns
12 Light Machine-guns
2 Light Anti-tank Rifles
2 Medium Mortars

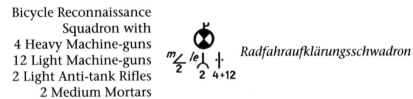

Radfahraufklärungsschwadron

The load capacity of transport columns, ferries and bridges are represented by the addition of a tonnage figure in or under the tactical symbol.

Example:

Transport Company (180
Ton Load Capacity)

180

Kraftfahrkompanie c (180 t)

Bridge with 40 Ton
Load Capacity

40

Brücke mit 40 t Tragfähigkeit

PART II
COMMAND AND SENIOR HEADQUARTERS

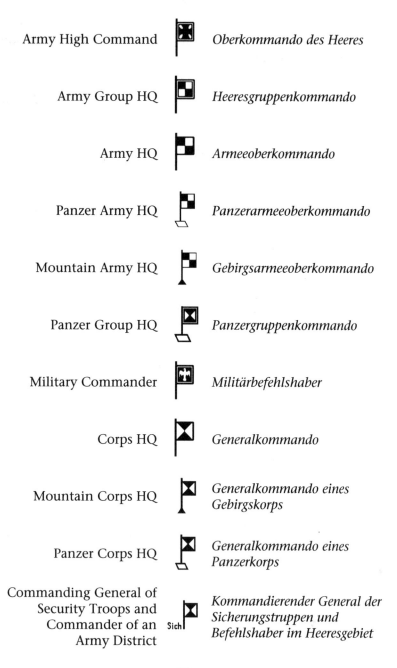

Army High Command   *Oberkommando des Heeres*

Army Group HQ   *Heeresgruppenkommando*

Army HQ   *Armeeoberkommando*

Panzer Army HQ   *Panzerarmeeoberkommando*

Mountain Army HQ   *Gebirgsarmeeoberkommando*

Panzer Group HQ   *Panzergruppenkommando*

Military Commander   *Militärbefehlshaber*

Corps HQ   *Generalkommando*

Mountain Corps HQ   *Generalkommando eines Gebirgskorps*

Panzer Corps HQ   *Generalkommando eines Panzerkorps*

Commanding General of Security Troops and Commander of an Army District   *Kommandierender General der Sicherungstruppen und Befehlshaber im Heeresgebiet*

Infantry Division HQ — *Kommando einer Infanteriedivision*

Divisional Group HQ — *Kommando einer Divisionsgruppe*

Jager / Light Infantry Division HQ — *Kommando einer Jägerdivision*

Mountain Division HQ — *Kommando einer Gebirgsdivision*

Panzer Division HQ — *Kommando einer Panzerdivision*

Panzergrenadier Division HQ — *Kommando einer Panzergrenadierdivision*

Cavalry Division HQ — *Kommando einer Kavalleriedividion*

Security Division HQ — *Kommando einer Sicherungsdivision*

Artillery Division HQ — *Kommando einer Artilleriedivision*

Artillery Division HQ z.b.V. or Senior Artillery Commander's HQ — *Artillerie-Divisionsstab z.b.V. oder Stab eines höheren Artillerie-Kommandeurs*

Senior Coastal Artillery Commander's HQ — *Stab eines höheren Küstenartilleriekommandeurs*

Military Mapping and Survey Commander's HQ — *Stab Kriegskarten und Vermessungschef*

HQ of a General of Engineers with an Army Group		*Stab eines Generals der Pioniere bei einer Heeresgruppe*
Inspector of Land Fortifications HQ		*Stab Inspekteur der Landesbefestigungen*
Fortifications HQ		*Kommandantur der Befestigungen*
Army Group Senior Signals Commander's HQ		*Stab eines Heeresgruppen bzw. höheren Nachrichtenführers*
Senior Signals Commander for Land Fortifications HQ		*Stab eines höheren Nachrichtenführers der Landesbefestigung*
HQ Senior Commander of Supply Troops		*Stab eines höheren Kommandeurs der Nachschubtruppen*
Commander of a Military Administrative District's HQ		*Stab Chef des Militärverwaltungsbezirks*
Army Ordnance Superintendent's HQ		*Stab Heeresfeldzeuginspizient*
Military Government Area HQ		*Oberfeldkommandantur*
HQ Commander of an Army's Rear Area		*Kommandant rückwärtiges Armeegebiet*
Infantry Brigade HQ / Brigade HQ		*Stab eines Infanteriekommandeurs, eines Brigadekommandeurs*
Panzer Brigade HQ		*Stab einer Panzerbrigade*

Cavalry Brigade HQ — *Stab einer Reiterbrigade*

Artillery Commander's HQ — *Stab eines Artilleriekommandeurs*

Coastal Artillery Commander's HQ — *Stab eines Küstenartilleriekommandeurs*

Fortress Artillery Commander's HQ — *Stab eines Festungsartilleriekommandeurs*

HQ Commander of Mapping and Surveying Troops / HQ Senior Officer of Military Maps and Surveying — *Stab eines Kommandeurs Karten und Vermessungstruppen bzw. Stab eines höheren Offiziers des Kriegskarten und Vermessungswesens*

General of Transportation's HQ — *Stab General des Transportwesens*

Army Engineer Commander's HQ — *Stab eines Armeepionierführers*

Fortress Engineer Commander's HQ — *Stab eines Festungspionierkommandeurs*

Senior Construction Engineer Commander's HQ — *Oberbaupionierstab*

HQ Commander of Motorised Rocket Launchers — *Stab eines Kommandeurs der Nebeltruppe (mot)*

Railway Engineer Brigade's HQ — *Stab einer Eisenbahnpionierbrigade*

Army Signals Commander's HQ — *Stab eines Armeenachrichtenführers*

HQ Operations Signals Troops — *Stab eines Kommandeurs Führungsnachrichtentruppen*

Panzer Army Signals Commander's HQ — *Stab eines Panzerarmeenachrichtenführers*

Commander of Army Supply Troops HQ — *Stab eines Kommandeurs der Armeenachschubtruppen*

Commander of Panzer Army Supply Troops HQ — *Stab eines Kommandeurs der Panzerarmeenachschubtruppen*

Senior Ordnance HQ — *Oberfeldzeugstab*

Commander of Vehicle Park Troops HQ — *Stab Kommandeur der Kraftfahrparktruppen*

Military Government HQ — *Feldkommandantur*

PART III

COMBAT TROOPS

INFANTRY

INFANTRY – HEADQUARTERS

Infantry Regiment HQ   *Stab eines Infanterieregiments*

Jager / Light Infantry
Regiment HQ   *Stab eines Jägerregiments*

Security Regiment HQ   *Stab eines Sicherungsregiments*

Bicycle-mounted Security
Regiment HQ   *Stab eines Radfahrsicherungsregiments*

Border Guard Regiment HQ   *Stab eines Grenzschutzregiments*

Regional Defence Regiment HQ   *Stab eines Landesschützenregiments*

Infantry Battalion HQ   *Stab eines Infanteriebataillons*

Divisional Fusilier Battalion HQ   *Stab eines Divisionsfüsilierbataillons*

Jager / Light Infantry
Battalion HQ   *Stab eines Jägerbataillons*

Security Battalion HQ   *Stab eines Sicherungsbataillons*

Border Guard Battalion HQ   *Stab eines Grenzschutzbataillons*

Regional Defence Battalion HQ	Ls▶	*Stab eines Landesschützenbataillons*
Bicycle-mounted Security Battalion HQ	Sich▶⊕	*Stab eines Sicherungsbataillons auf Fahrrädern*
Infantry Company Commander	⌐	*Führer einer Infanteriekompanie*
Commander of a Company of Bicycle Troops	⌐⊕	*Führer einer Radfahrkompanie*

INFANTRY – UNITS

Infantry Company	▭	*Infanterie Kompanie*
Infantry Company on Bicycles	▭⊗	*Infanteriekompanie auf Fahrrädern*
Jager / Light Infantry Company	Jg ▭	*Jägerkompanie*
Security Company	Sich▭	*Sicherungskompanie*
Border Guard Company	Gr▭	*Grenzschutzkompanie*
Regional Protection Company	Ls▭	*Landesschützenkompanie*
Field Convalescent Company	▭G	*Feldgenesendenkompanie*
Machine-gun Company	▭+	*Maschinengewehrkompanie*
Jager / Light Infantry Machine-gun Company	Jg▭+	*Jägermaschinengewehrkompanie*

Border Protection Machine-gun Company	Gr⬚✚⬚	*Grenzschutzmaschinengewehr-kompanie*
Company of Bicycle Troops	⊗	*Radfahrkompanie*
Bicycle-mounted Security Company	Sich ⊗	*Sicherungsradfahrkompanie*
Infantry Gun Company	⊥	*Infanteriegeschützkompanie*
Part-motorised Infantry Gun Company	⊥	*Infanteriegeschützkompanie (tmot)*
Infantry Anti-tank Company	⊤	*Infanteriepanzerjägerkompanie*
Part-motorised Infantry Anti-tank Company	⊤	*Infanteriepanzerjägerkompanie (tmot)*
Mortar Company	◺	*Granatwerferkompanie*
HQ Company	st	*Stabskompanie*
Mortar Platoon	◺	*Granatwerferzug*
Infantry Gun Platoon	⊥	*Infanteriegeschützzug*
Infantry Mounted Platoon	◿	*Infanteriereiterzug*
HQ Signals / Communications Platoon	⌐⌐	*Nachrichtenzug bei Stäben*
Infantry Field Engineer Platoon	J	*Infanteriepionierzug*

Infantry Sound Ranging Troop   **J Sich**   *Infanterieschallmeßtrupp*

INFANTRY – WEAPONS

Light Mortar, up to 7.9cm calibre	*le* ∠	*leichter Granatwerfer bis 7.9cm*
Medium Mortar, 8–11.9cm calibre	*m* ∠	*mittlerer Granatwerfer 8–11.9cm*
Heavy Mortar, 12cm calibre or above	*s* ∠	*schwerer Granatwerfer ab 12cm*
Light Infantry Gun, up to 7.5cm calibre	*le* ⊥	*leichtes Infanteriegeschütz bis 7.5cm*
Heavy Infantry Gun, 7.6cm calibre or above	*s* ⊥	*schweres Infanteriegeschütz ab 7.6cm*
Anti-tank Rifle	⅄	*Panzerbüchse*
Heavy Anti-tank Rifle	*s* ⅄	*schwere Panzerbüchse*
Light Anti-tank Gun, up to 3.9cm calibre	*le* ⊤	*leichte Panzerjägerkanone bis 3.9cm*
Medium Anti-tank Gun, 4–5.9cm calibre	*m* ⊤	*mittlerer Panzerjägerkanone 4–5.9cm*
Heavy Anti-tank Gun, 6–8.9cm calibre	*s* ⊤	*schwerer Panzerjägerkanone 6–8.9cm*

Super Heavy Anti-tank Gun, 9cm calibre or above	ᵚᵂ⊤	*schwerste Panzerjägerkanone ab 9cm*
Light Anti-aircraft Gun, up to 3.6cm calibre	*le*↑	*leichte Flakgeschütz bis 3.(*
Medium Anti-aircraft Gun, 3.7–5.9cm calibre	*m*↑	*mittlerer Flakgeschüt*
Heavy Anti-aircraft Gun, 6–15.9cm calibre	*s*↑	*schwerer Flakgeschütz 6–1⁵.*
Super Heavy Anti-aircraft Gun, 16cm calibre or above	*ᵚᵂ*↑	*schwerste Flakgeschütz ab 16cm*

Examples of more detailed infantry weapon designations:

8cm Mortar	₈$\angle$¹ˑ⁹	*8cm Granatwerfer*
12cm Mortar	₁₂$\angle$⁶ˑ⁰	*12cm Granatwerfer*
7.5cm Infantry Gun	₇ˌ₅⌐³ˑ⁵	*7.5cm Infanteriegeschütz*
15cm Infantry Gun	₁₅⌐⁴ˑ⁷	*15cm Infanteriegeschütz*
2.8cm Anti-tank Rifle	₂ˌ₈⋏	*2.8cm Panzerbüchse*
3.7cm Anti-tank Gun	₃ˌ₇⊤	*3.7cm Panzerjägerkanone*
5cm Anti-tank Gun	₅⊤	*5cm Panzerjägerkanone*
2cm Anti-aircraft Gun	₂↑⁴ˑ⁸	*2cm Flakgeschütz*
Quadruple 2cm Anti-aircraft Gun	ᵥᵢₑᵣₗ²↑⁴ˑ⁸	*2cm Flakgeschütz (Vierling)*

INFANTRY – ORGANISATION

An organisational example:
Infantry Battalion
consisting of: HQ, 3
Infantry Companies,
each including: 12 Light
Machine-Guns, 3 Heavy
Mortars, 3 Anti-tank
Rifles, 1 Machine-Gun
Company with:
12 Heavy Machine-guns,
6 Heavy Mortars

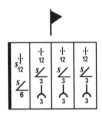

*Infanteriebataillon zu
1 Stab, 3 Infanteriekom-
panien mit je 12 le M. G.,
3 s Gr. W., 3 Panzer-
büchsen, 1 Maschinen-
gewehrkompanie mit 12s
M. G., 6 sGr. W.*

Examples of symbols as they would appear on maps:

1st Battalion of the 21st
Infantry Regiment

Infanteriebataillon I. /21

March Column of Infantry
Units, the arrow indicating
direction of march

*Marschkolonne von
Infanterieeinheiten*

MOUNTAIN INFANTRY

MOUNTAIN INFANTRY – HEADQUARTERS

Mountain Infantry
Regiment HQ

Stab eines Gebirgsjägerregiments

Mountain Infantry
Battalion HQ

Stab eines Gebirgsjägerbataillons

High Mountain Battalion HQ

Stab eines Hochgebirgsbataillons

Mountain Infantry
Company Commander

*Führer einer
Gebirgsjägerkompanie*

MOUNTAIN INFANTRY – UNITS

Mountain Infantry Company   *Gebirgsjägerkompanie*

Mountain Infantry
Machine-gun Company   *Gebirgsjägermaschinengewehr-kompanie*

HQ Company of a Mountain
Infantry Regiment   *Stabskompanie eines Gebirgsjägerregiments*

Heavy Weapons Company of a
Mountain Infantry Battalion   *Schwere Kompanie eines Gebirgsjägerbataillons*

Towed Mountain
Anti-aircraft Company   *Gebirgsfliegerabwehrkompanie (mot Z)*

Towed Mountain
Anti-tank Company   *Gebirgspanzerjägerkompanie (mot Z)*

Light Mountain Gun Platoon   *leichter Gebirgsinfanteriegeschützzug*

Mountain Mortar Platoon   *Gebirgsgranatwerferzug*

Mountain Sound Ranging Unit   *Gebirgsschallmeßtrupp*

Light Mountain
Transport Column   *leichte Gebirgsjägerkolonne*

MOUNTAIN INFANTRY – ORGANISATION

An organisational example:
Mountain Infantry
Battalion consisting of:
HQ,
3 Mountain Infantry
Companies each
including:
12 Light Machine-guns,
2 Heavy Machine-guns,
3 Light Anti-tank Rifles,
3 Heavy Mortars
1 Mountain Infantry
Machine-gun Company
with 12 Heavy Machine-
guns, 1 HQ Company of:
1 Engineer Platoon, incl. 4
Light Machine-guns,
1 Signals Platoon,
1 Mountain Infantry Gun
Platoon with 2 Light
Mountain Infantry Guns

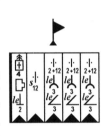

Gebirgsjägerbataillons zu
1 Stab
3 Gebirgsjägerkompanie mit
je 12 le M. G., 2 s M. G., 3 le
Pz.B., 3 s Gr. W.
Gebirgsjägermaschinengewehr-
kompanie mit 12s M. G.
1 Stabskompanie mit:
1 Pionierzug zu 4 le M. G.,
1 Nachrichtenzug,
1 Gebirgsinfanteriegeschütz-
zug zu 2 le Geb. I. G.

Examples of symbols as they would appear on maps:

1st Battalion of the 98th
Mountain Infantry Regiment

Gebirgsjägerbataillons I. /98

March Column of Mountain
Infantry Units, the arrow
indicating direction of march

Marschkolonne von
Gebirgsjägereinheiten

PANZERTRUPPEN

PANZERTRUPPEN – HEADQUARTERS

Panzer Regiment HQ   *Stab eines Panzerregiments*

Panzer Battalion HQ   *Stab eines Panzerbataillons*

Panzer Company HQ   *Stab eines Panzerkompanie*

Commander of a Platoon of
Flamethrower Panzers   *Führer einer Panzerflammzuges*

PANZERTRUPPEN – UNITS

Light Panzer Company   *leichte Panzerkompanie*

Light Panzer Platoon   *leichte Panzerzug*

Medium Panzer Company   *mittlere Panzerkompanie*

Heavy Panzer Company   *schwere Panzerkompanie*

HQ Company, Panzer Battalion   *Stabskompanie einer
Panzerabteilung*

Panzer Workshop Company   *Panzerwerkstattkompanie*

Flamethrower Panzer Platoon   *Panzerflammzug*

Panzer Workshop Platoon   *Panzerwerkstattzug*

Panzer Recovery Unit   *Panzerbergetrupp*

Signals Platoon for a
Panzer Unit   *Nachrichtenzug eines
Panzerverbandes*

Supplies and Administration
Section of a Panzer Battalion   *Staffel für Nachschub und
Verwaltung einer Panzerabteilung*

Armoured Train   *Panzerzug*

PANZERTRUPPEN – VEHICLES

Panzerkampfwagen II   *Panzerkampfwagen II*

Flame-throwing Panzer   *F-Panzerkampfwagen*

Panzerkampfwagen III   *Panzerkampfwagen III*

Command Panzer   *Panzerbefehlswagen*

Bridge-laying Panzer   *Panzerkampfwagen-Brückenleger*

PANZERTRUPPEN – ORGANISATION

An organisational example:

Panzer Battalion consisting of:		*Panzerabteilung zu*
HQ		*1 Stab*
HQ Company		*1 Stabskompanie*
3 Medium Panzer Companies		*3 mittleren Panzerkompanien*
1 Workshop Company		*1 Werkstattkompanie*

Examples of symbols as they would appear on maps:

1st Battalion of the 6th Panzer Regiment   *Panzerbataillons I. /6*

March Column of Panzer Units, arrow indicating direction of movement   *Marschkolonne von Panzereinheiten*

MOTORISED INFANTRY and PANZERGRENADIERS – HEADQUARTERS

N.b. throughout this section, 'unarmoured' usually denotes the unit is equipped with trucks, 'armoured' indicates the use of half-tracked armoured personnel carriers, e.g. SdKfz 251.

Motorised Infantry Regiment HQ or Panzergrenadier Regiment HQ (Unarmoured)		*Stab eines Infanterieregiments (mot) oder Panzergrenadier-regiment (ungepanzert)*
Panzergrenadier Regiment HQ (Armoured)		*Stab Panzergrenadierregiment (gp)*
Motorised Infantry Battalion HQ or Panzergrenadier Battalion HQ (Unarmoured)		*Stab eines Infanteriebataillons (mot) oder Panzergrenadier-bataillon (ungepanzert)*
Panzergrenadier Battalion HQ (Armoured)		*Stab Panzergrenadierbataillon (gp)*
Motorised Machine-gun Battalion HQ		*Stab eines Maschinengewehr-bataillons (mot)*

Motorised Mortar Battalion HQ — *Stab eines Granatwerferbataillons (mot)*

HQ Towed Anti-aircraft Battalion — *Stab eines Fliegerabwehrbataillons (mot Z)*

Self-Propelled Anti-aircraft Battalion HQ — *Stab eines Fliegerabwehrbataillons (Sf)*

Motorcycle Infantry Battalion HQ — *Stab eines Kraftradschützenbataillons*

Commander, Motorised Infantry Company or Commander, Panzergrenadier Company (Unarmoured) — *Führer einer Infanteriekompanie (mot) oder Panzergrenadier-kompanie (ungepanzert)*

Commander, Panzergrenadier Company (Armoured) — *Führer einer Panzergrenadierkompanie (gp)*

Commander, Motorcycle Infantry Company — *Führer einer Kraftradschützenkompanie*

MOTORISED INFANTRY and PANZERGRENADIERS – UNITS

Motorised Infantry Company or Panzergrenadier Company (Unarmoured) — *Infanteriekompanie (mot) oder Panzergrenadierkompanie (ungepanzert)*

Panzergrenadier Company (Armoured) — *Panzergrenadierkompanie (gp)*

Infantry Company in Volkswagens — *Infanteriekompanie auf Volkswagen*

Motorcycle Infantry Company — *Kraftradschützenkompanie*

Infantry Company on Half-track Motorcycles — *Infanteriekompanie auf Kettenkrad*

Motorised Machine-gun Company — *Maschinengewehrkompanie (mot)*

Motorised Mortar Company		*Granatwerferkompanie (mot)*
Motorcycle Machine-gun Company		*Kraftradmaschinengewehr-kompanie*
Towed Infantry Gun Company		*Infanteriegeschützkompanie (mot Z)*
Self-propelled Heavy Infantry Gun Company		*schwere Infanteriegeschütz-kompanie (Sf)*
Towed Infantry Anti-tank Company		*Infanteriepanzerjägerkompanie (mot Z)*
Towed 2cm Anti-aircraft Gun Company		*Fliegerabwehrkompanie 2cm (mot Z)*
Self-propelled 2cm Anti-aircraft Gun Company		*Fliegerabwehrkompanie 2cm (Sf)*
Towed 3.7cm Anti-aircraft Gun Company		*Fliegerabwehrkompanie 3,7cm (mot Z)*
Motorised Heavy Weapons Company		*schwere Kompanie (mot)*
Heavy Weapons Company of a Panzergrenadier Battalion (Armoured)		*schwere Kompanie eines Panzergrenadierbataillons (gp)*
Heavy Weapons Company of a Motorcycle Infantry Battalion		*schwere Kompanie eines Kraftradschützenbataillons*
Heavy Weapons Company on Half-track Motorcycles		*schwere Kompanie auf Kettenkrad*
Motorised HQ Company		*Stabskompanie (mot)*
HQ Company of a Panzergrenadier Regiment (Armoured)		*Stabskompanie eines Panzergrenadierregiments (gp)*

Motorised Mortar Platoon   *Granatwerferzug (mot)*

Towed Light Infantry
Gun Platoon   *leichter Infanteriegeschützzug (mot Z)*

Towed Heavy Infantry
Gun Platoon   *schwerer Infanteriegeschützzug (mot Z)*

Self-propelled Heavy Infantry
Gun Platoon   *schwerer Infanteriegeschützzug (Sf)*

Towed Infantry
Anti-tank Platoon   *Infanteriepanzerjägerzug (mot Z)*

Motorised Infantry Field
Engineer Platoon   *Infanteriepionierzug (mot)*

Motorised Signals Platoon   *Nachrichtenzug (mot)*

Motorcycle Infantry Platoon   *Kraftradschützenzug*

Motorcycle Messenger Platoon   *Kraftradmeldezug*

Motorised Infantry Sound
Ranging Unit   *Infanterieschallmeßtrupp (mot)*

MOTORISED INFANTRY and PANZERGRENADIERS – ORGANISATION

Organisational examples:
Motorised Infantry
Battalion consisting of:
HQ
3 Infantry Companies,
each including: 12 Light
Machine-guns, 6 Heavy
Machine-guns, 3 Light
Anti-tank Rifles, 1 Heavy
Anti-tank Rifles, 3 Heavy
Mortars
Machine-Gun Company
with: 12 Heavy Machine-
guns, 3 Light Anti-tank
Guns, 6 Heavy Mortars

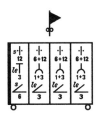

Infanteriebataillon (mot)
zu
1 Stab
3 Infanteriekompanie mit je
12 le M. G., 6 s M. G.,
3 le Pz. B., 1 s Pz. B.,
3 s Gr. W.
Maschinengewehr-
kompanie mit 12s M. G.,
3 le Pak, 6 s Gr, W.

Panzergrenadier Battalion
consisting of:
HQ
3 Panzergrenadier
Companies (Armoured),
each including: 18 Light
Machine-guns, 2 Medium
Mortars, 3 Light Anti-
tank Guns
Panzergrenadier Heavy
Weapons Company,
including: 8 Light
Infantry Guns, 3 Heavy
Anti-tank Guns, 6
Flamethrowers, 13 Light
Machine-guns and 1
Field Engineer platoon

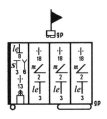

Panzergrenadierbataillon
(gp) zu
1 Stab
3 Panzergrenadier-
kompanie (gp) mit je 18 le
M. G., 2 m Gr. W., 3 le
Pak.
schwere Panzergrenadier-
kompanie mit 8 le I. G., 3 s
Pak, 6 Flammenwerfer, 13
le M. G. und 1 Pionierzug

Examples of symbols as they would appear on maps:

1st (Motorised) Battalion of the 15th Infantry Regiment   *Infanteriebataillon (mot) I./15*

1st (Armoured) Battalion of the 3rd Panzergrenadier Regiment   *Panzergrenadierbataillon (gp) I./3*

March Column of Motorised Infantry Units   *Marschkolonne von Infanterieeinheiten (mot)*

March Column of Panzergrenadier Units (Armoured)   *Marschkolonne von Panzergrenadiereinheiten (gp)*

ANTI-TANK TROOPS – HEADQUARTERS

Anti-tank Battalion HQ   *Stab einer Panzerjägerabteilung*

Self-propelled Anti-tank Battalion HQ   *Stab einer Panzerjägerabteilung (Sf)*

Anti-tank Company Commander   *Führer einer Panzerjägerkompanie*

Commander of a Self-propelled Anti-tank Company   *Führer einer Panzerjägerkompanie (Sf)*

ANTI-TANK TROOPS – UNITS

Towed Anti-tank Company   *Panzerjägerkompanie (mot Z)*

Part-motorised Anti-tank Company   *Panzerjägerkompanie (tmot)*

Towed Anti-tank Platoon   *Panzerjägerzug (mot Z)*

Self-propelled Anti-tank Company   *Panzerjägerkompanie (Sf)*

Self-propelled Anti-tank platoon   *Panzerjägerzug (Sf)*

ANTI-TANK TROOPS – WEAPONS

Light Anti-tank gun, up to 3.9cm calibre   *leichte Panzerjägerkanone bis 3.9cm*

Medium Anti-tank gun, 4–5.9cm calibre   *mittlere Panzerjägerkanone 4– 5.9cm*

Heavy Anti-tank gun 6–8.9cm, calibre   *schwere Panzerjägerkanone 6 – 8.9cm*

Super Heavy Anti-tank gun, 9cm calibre or above   *schwerste Panzerjägerkanone ab 9cm*

Examples of more detailed anti-tank weapon designations:

5cm Anti-tank gun M38 ('Pak 38')   *5cm Panzerjägerkanone 38*

4.7 cm Anti-tank gun (Czech origin)   *4.7 cm Panzerjägerkanone (tschechisch)*

ANTI-TANK TROOPS – ORGANISATION

Organisational example:

Self-propelled Anti-tank
Battalion consisting of:
HQ
Signals Platoon
3 Heavy Anti-tank
companies, each with:
10 8.8cm Self-propelled
Anti-tank guns

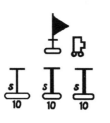

*Panzerjägerabteilung (Sf)
zu
1 Stab mit
Nachrichtenzug (mot),
3 Panzerjägerkompanie
mit je 10 8.8cm
Panzerjägerkanone*

Examples of symbols as they would appear on maps:

166th Anti-tank Battalion *Panzerjägerabteilung 166*

March Column of Anti-tank
Units, arrow indicating
direction of movement
*Marschkolonne von
Panzerjägereinheiten*

PANZER RECONNAISSANCE UNITS – HEADQUARTERS

Panzer Reconnaissance
Regiment HQ

*Stab eines Panzeraufklärungs-
regiments*

Panzer Reconnaissance
Battalion HQ

*Stab eines Panzeraufklärungs-
abteilung*

Commander of a Panzer
Reconnaissance Company
*Führer einer Panzeraufklärungs-
kompanie*

PANZER RECONNAISSANCE UNITS – UNITS

Panzer Reconnaissance
Company, equipped with
4-wheel Armoured Cars
 Panzerspähkompanie

Panzer Reconnaissance Company, equipped with 8-wheel Armoured Cars   *Panzerspähkompanie a*

Panzer Reconnaissance Company, equipped with Tanks   *Panzerspähkompanie b*

Panzer Reconnaissance Company, equipped with Half-tracks   *Panzerspähkompanie c*

Panzer Reconnaissance Company, equipped with Armoured Personnel Carriers   *Panzeraufklärungskompanie auf Schützenpanzerwagen*

Reconnaissance Company, equipped with Volkswagens   *Aufklärungskompanie auf Volkswagen*

Heavy Weapons Company of a Panzer Reconnaissance Battalion, equipped with Armoured Personnel Carriers   *schwere Kompanie einer Panzeraufklärungsabteilung auf Schützenpanzerwagen*

HQ Company of a Panzer Reconnaissance Regiment, equipped with Armoured Personnel Carriers   *Stabskompanie einer Panzeraufklärungsregiments auf Schützenpanzerwagen*

Light Transport Column of a Panzer Reconnaissance Battalion   *leichte Kolonne einer Panzeraufklärungsabteilung*

PANZER RECONNAISSANCE UNITS – EQUIPMENT

Light Armoured Car   *leichter Panzerspähwagen*

Light Armoured Car (French origin)   *leichter Panzerspähwagen (französisch)*

Light Reconnaissance Half-track (Command Vehicle w/Radio)   *leichter Panzerspähwagen (Halbkette) (Fu)*

Light Reconnaissance Panzer (Command Vehicle w/Radio)   *leichter Panzerspähwagen (Vollkette) (Fu)*

Heavy Armoured Car
(8-wheel)

*schwerer Panzerspähwagen
(8 Rad)*

Heavy Armoured Car
(8-wheel) (Command
Version w/Radio)

*schwerer Panzerspähwagen
(8 Rad) (Fu)*

PANZER RECONNAISSANCE UNITS – ORGANISATION

Organisational example:
Panzer Reconnaissance
Battalion consisting of:
1 HQ,
1 Panzer Reconnaissance
Company with Armoured
Personnel Carriers,
1 Panzer Reconnaissance
Company with Half-
tracks,
1 Panzer Reconnaissance
Company with 4-wheel
Armoured Cars,
1 Heavy Weapons
Company with Armoured
Personal Carriers,
1 Light Transport
Column

*Panzeraufklärungs-
abteilung zu
1 Stab,
1 Panzerspähkompanie,
1 Panzerspähkompanie c,
1 Panzeraufklärungs-
kompanie auf Schützen-
panzerwagen,
1 schwere Kompanie auf
Schützenpanzerwagen,
1 leichte Kolonne*

Examples of symbols as they would appear on maps:

3rd Panzer Reconnaissance
Battalion

Panzeraufklärungsabteilung 3

March Column of Panzer
Reconnaissance Units, arrow
indicating direction of
movement

*Marschkolonne von
Panzeraufklärungseinheiten*

44

CAVALRY

CAVALRY – HEADQUARTERS

Cavalry Regiment HQ   *Stab eines Reiterregiments*

Cavalry Battalion HQ   *Stab eines Reiterabteilung*

Cavalry Squadron Commander   *Führer einer Reiterschwadron*

CAVALRY – UNITS

Cavalry Squadron   *Reiterschwadron*

Cavalry Machine-gun Squadron   *Kavalleriemaschinengewehr-schwadron*

HQ Squadron of a Cavalry Regiment   *Stabschwadron eines Reiterregiments*

Heavy Weapons Squadron of a Cavalry Battalion   *schwerer Schwadron einer Reiterabteilung*

Cavalry Signals Platoon   *Kavallerienachrichtenzug*

Cavalry Gun Platoon   *Kavalleriegeschützzug*

Cavalry Anti-tank Platoon   *Kavalleriepanzerjägerzug*

Cavalry Field Engineer Platoon   *Kavalleriepionierzug*

Cavalry Mortar Platoon   *Kavalleriegranatwerferzug*

Examples of symbols as they would appear on maps:

1st Battalion of the 22nd
Cavalry Regiment   *Reiterabteilung I./22*

March Column of Cavalry
Units, arrow indicating
direction of movement   *Marschkolonne von
Kavallerieeinheiten*

ARTILLERY

ARTILLERY – HEADQUARTERS

Artillery Regiment HQ   *Stab eines Artillerieregiments*

Mountain Artillery Regiment
HQ   *Stab eines
Gebirgsartillerieregiments*

Motorised Artillery Regiment
HQ   *Stab eines Artillerieregiments
(mot)*

Panzer Artillery Regiment HQ   *Stab eines
Panzerartillerieregiments*

Railway Artillery Regiment HQ   *Stab eines
Eisenbahnartillerieregiments*

Light Artillery Battalion HQ   *Stab einer leichten
Artillerieabteilung*

Motorised Artillery
Battalion HQ   *Stab einer Artillerieabteilung
(mot)*

Panzer Artillery Battalion HQ

*Stab einer
Panzerartillerieabteilung*

Mountain Artillery
Battalion HQ

*Stab einer
Gebirgsartillerieabteilung*

Coastal Artillery Battalion HQ

*Stab einer
Küstenartillerieabteilung*

Fortress Artillery Battalion HQ

*Stab einer
Festungsartillerieabteilung*

Motorised Assault Gun
Battalion HQ

*Stab einer
Sturmgeschützabteilung (mot)*

Self-Propelled Artillery
Battalion HQ

Stab einer Artillerieabteilung (Sf)

Railway Artillery Battalion HQ

*Stab einer
Eisenbahnartillerieabteilung*

Motorised Anti-aircraft
Battalion HQ

Stab einer Flakabteilung (mot)

ARTILLERY – UNITS

Field Guns / Cannon

Light Gun Battery,
up to 9.9cm calibre

leichte Kanonenbatterie bis 9,9cm

Heavy Gun Battery,
10–20.9cm calibre

*schwere Kanonenbatterie
10–20,9cm*

Super Heavy Gun Battery, 21cm calibre or above schwerste Kanonenbatterie ab 21cm

Field guns / cannon – more detailed examples:

Light Battery with F.K. 18 Gun Batterie le F. K. 18

Battery with M15 Mountain Gun Batterie Geb. Kanone 15

Assault Gun Battery with 7.5cm Cannon Sturmgeschützbatterie (mot) 7,5cm K.

Towed 15cm K.18 Gun Battery Batterie 15cm K. 18 (mot Z)

24cm K. 556 Battery under Concrete Protection, which is under construction (guns of French origin) Batterie 24cm K. 556 (f) unter Beton im Bau

Howitzers

Light Howitzer Battery, up to 9.9cm calibre leichte Haubitzbatterie bis 9,9cm

Heavy Howitzer Battery, 10–20.9cm calibre schwere Haubitzbatterie 10 – 20,9cm

Super Heavy Howitzer Battery, 21cm calibre or above schwerste Haubitzbatterie ab 21cm

Howitzers – more detailed examples:

Towed Battery with M18 Light Field Howitzers Batterie le F. H. 18 (mot Z)

Self-Propelled Battery with M18 Light Field Howitzers *Batterie le F. H. 18 (Sf)*

Mortars

Heavy Mortar Battery, 10–20.9cm calibre *schwere Mörserbatterie 10–20,9cm*

Super Heavy Mortar Battery, 21cm calibre or above *schwerste Mörserbatterie ab 21cm*

Mortars – more detailed examples:

Towed Battery with 21cm M18 Mortars *Batterie 21 cm Wrf. 18 (mot Z)*

Coastal Battery with 22cm M531 (static) Mortars (of French origin) *Küst – Battr. 22cm Wrf. 531 (ortsfest) Frankreich*

Battery with 30.5cm M633 Mortars (of British origin) *Battr. 30,5cm Wrf. 633 (E) England*

Anti-aircraft Artillery

Light Anti-aircraft Battery, up to 3.6cm calibre *leichte Flakbatterie bis 3,6cm*

Medium Anti-aircraft Battery, 3.7–5.9 cm calibre *mittlere Flakbatterie 3,7–5,9cm*

Heavy Anti-aircraft Battery, 6–15.9cm calibre — *schwere Flakbatterie 6–15,9cm*

Super Heavy Anti-aircraft Battery, 16cm calibre or above — *schwerste Flakbatterie ab 16cm*

Towed Anti-Aircraft 60cm Searchlight Section — *Flakscheinwerferstaffel (mot Z) (60cm)*

Anti-aircraft Artillery – more detailed examples:

Motorised 2cm Anti-aircraft Battery — *Flakbatterie 2cm (mot Z)*

8.8 cm Anti-aircraft Battery mounted on Railway Flatbed Cars — *Flakbatterie 8,8cm (E)*

HQ Battery of an Artillery Regiment or Battalion — *Stabsbatterie eines Artillerieregiments oder Abteilung*

HQ Battery of a Mountain Artillery Regiment or Battalion — *Stabsbatterie eines Gebirgsartillerieregiments oder Abteilung*

Motorised HQ Battery of a Motorised Artillery Regiment or Motorised Battalion — *Stabsbatterie (mot) eines Artillerieregiments (mot) oder Abteilung (mot)*

Motorised HQ Battery of a Armoured Panzer Regiment or Battalion — *Stabsbatterie (mot) eines Panzerartillerieregiments oder Abteilung*

Motorised HQ Battery of an Assault Gun Battalion — *Stabsbatterie (mot) einer Sturmgeschützabteilung (mot)*

Self-propelled HQ Battery of a Self-propelled Artillery Regiment or a Self-propelled Battalion — *Stabsbatterie (Sf) eines Artillerieregiments (Sf) oder Abteilung (Sf)*

Motorised HQ Battery of a Motorised Anti-aircraft Battalion		*Stabsbatterie (mot) einer Flakabteilung (mot)*
Light Artillery Column		*leichte Artilleriekolonne*
Motorised Light Artillery Column		*leichte Artilleriekolonne (mot)*
Artillery Prime-mover Section, equipped with German vehicles		*Art.-Kraftzugstaffel d*
Pack Animal Section, Light Artillery Battalion of a Mountain Division		*Tragtierstaffel einer leichten Artillerieabteilung einer Gebirgsdivision*
Pack Animal Section, Heavy Artillery Battalion of a Mountain Division		*Tragtierstaffel einer schweren Artillerieabteilung einer Gebirgsdivision*
Motorised Light Anti-aircraft Column		*leicht Flakkolonne (mot)*
Motorised Heavy Velocity-Measuring Platoon[1]		*schwerer Vo-Meßzug (mot)*
Motorised Light Velocity-Measuring Unit[2]		*leicht Vo-Meßtrupp (mot)*
Artillery Mapping and Survey Unit		*Artillerievermessungstrupp*

1 Used by heavy artillery (usually super-heavy siege guns) to measure muzzle velocity.
2 As above, but used by field artillery.

Some other artillery unit symbols:

Observation Post *Beobachtungsstelle*

Location of Ammunition
Caissons, Limbers, etc. *Protzenstellung*

HQ Battery *Stabsbatterie*

Examples of symbols as they would appear on maps:

1st Battalion (Light Field
Howitzer) of the 1st Artillery
Regiment *Abteilung leichte Feldhaubitzen
I. /A. R. 1*

1st Battalion (Heavy Field
Howitzer) of the 37th Artillery
Regiment in position *Abteilung schwere Feldhaubitzen
I. /A. R. 37 in Stellung*

March Column of Artillery
Units, arrow indicating
direction of movement *Marschkolonne von
Artillerieeinheiten*

RECONNAISSANCE ARTILLERY – HEADQUARTERS

Motorised Light Observation
Battalion HQ *Stab einer leichten
Beobachtungsabteilung (mot)*

Motorised Light Mountain
Observation Battalion HQ *Stab einer leichten Gebirgsbeobachtungsabteilung (mot)*

HQ Part-mobile
Observation Battalion *Stab einer Beobachtungsabteilung
(t bew.)*

RECONNAISSANCE ARTILLERY – UNITS

Motorised HQ Battery of a Motorised Light Observation Battalion
Stabsbatterie (mot) einer leichten Beobachtungsabteilung (mot)

Motorised HQ Battery of a Motorised Light Mountain Observation Battalion
Stabsbatterie (mot) einer leichten Gebirgsbeobachtungsabteilung (mot)

Motorised Panzer Observation Battery
Beobachtungsbatterie (mot) (Pz)

Motorised Flash Ranging Battery
Lichtmeßbatterie (mot)

Motorised Flash Ranging Battery with a Balloon Platoon
Lichtmeßbatterie (mot) mit Ballonzug

Part-motorised Sound Ranging Battery
Schallmeßbatterie (tmot)

Motorised Mountain Sound Ranging Battery
Gebirgsschallmeßbatterie (mot)

Motorised Metereological Section
Wetterzug (mot)

Reinforced Motorised Metereological Section
Verst. Wetterzug (mot)

Motorised Ranging Unit
Meßertrupp (mot)

Motorised Survey and Ranging Platoon
Vermessungs- und Einschießzug (mot)

Motorised Balloon Platoon   *Ballonzug (mot)*

Pack Animal Section of a Light
Mountain Observation
Battalion   *Tragtierstaffel einer leichten
Gebirgsbeobachtungsabteilung*

RECONNAISSANCE ARTILLERY – OTHER

Flash Ranging Station *Lichtmeßstelle*

Sound Ranging Station *Schallmeßstelle*

Early Warning Station *Vorwarnerstelle*

Light Interpretation /
Observation Position[3] *Auswertungsstelle Licht*

Sound Interpretation Position[4] *Auswertungsstelle Schall*

---

3   Observed light flashes from artillery and plotted their positions by triangulation.
4   As above, but via sound.

RECONNAISSANCE ARTILLERY – ORGANISATION

Organisational example:
Light Observation
Battalion with Balloon
Platoon:
HQ
1 HQ Battery with 2
Light Machine-guns,
1 Sound-Ranging Battery
with 9 Light Machine-
guns,
1 Flash-Ranging Battery
with Balloon Platoon,
2 Anti-aircraft Guns,
6 Light Machine-guns

leichte
Beobachtungsabteilung mit
Ballonzug zu
1 Stab
1 Stabsbatterie mit 2 le
M.G.,
1 Schallmeßbatterie mit
9 le M. G.,
1 Lichtmeßbatterie mit
Ballonzug mit 2
Flakgeschützen, 6 le M. G.

Examples of symbols as they would appear on maps:

30th Observation Battalion   *Beobachtungsabteilung 30*

ROCKET LAUNCHER / NEBELWERFER TROOPS

ROCKET LAUNCHER / NEBELWERFER TROOPS – HEADQUARTERS

Motorised HQ of a Regiment of
Nebelwerfer Troops

Stab eines Regiments der
Nebeltruppe (mot)

Motorised HQ of a Battalion of
Nebelwerfer Troops

Stab eines Abteilung der
Nebeltruppe (mot)

Motorised HQ of a
Decontamination Battalion
Stab eines Entgiftungsabteilung
(mot)

ROCKET LAUNCHER / NEBELWERFER TROOPS – UNITS

Light Rocket Launcher, up to 10.9 cm calibre

leichter Nebelwerfer bis 10,9 cm

Medium Rocket Launcher, 11–15.9 cm calibre

mittlerer Nebelwerfer 11–15,9 cm

Heavy Rocket Launcher, 16–21.9cm calibre

schwerer Nebelwerfer 16–21,9 cm

Super Heavy Rocket Launcher, 22 cm calibre or above

schwerster Nebelwerfer ab 22 cm

Some examples:

Towed Battery with M40 Rocket Launchers

Batterie Nebelwerfer 40 (mot Z)

Towed Battery with M41 Rocket Launchers

Batterie Nebelwerfer 41 (mot Z)

Motorised HQ Battery of a Regiment and of a Battalion of Nebelwerfer Troops

Stabsbatterie (mot) eines Regiments und einer Abteilung der Nebeltruppe

Motorised Light Rocket Launcher Column

leichte Werferkolonne (mot)

Motorised Light Rocket Launcher Transport Column for a Heavy Rocket Launcher Regiment

leichte Werferkolonne (s) (mot) für schweres Werferregiments

ROCKET LAUNCHER / NEBELWERFER TROOPS – ORGANISATION

Organisational examples:

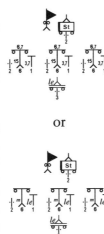

Motorised Rocket Launcher Battalion with: HQ with HQ Battery, incl. 2 Light Machine-guns, 3 Batteries, each with: 6 x 15cm M41 Rocket Launchers, 1 x 3.7 cm Anti-tank Gun, 2 x Light Machine-guns, 1 Light Rocket Launcher Transport Column, incl. 3 Light Machine-guns

or

Werferabteilung (mot) zu 1 Stab mit Stabsbatterie mit 2 le M.G., 3 Batterien mit je 6 15cm Nebelwerfer 41, 1 3,7 cm Pak, 2 le M.G., 1 le Werferkolonne mit 3 le M. G.

SURVEY AND MAPPING TROOPS

Motorised Mapping Battery or Motorised Light Map Printing Unit

Kartenbatterie (mot) oder leichte Kartendruckereiabteilung (mot)

Motorised Mapping Platoon

Kartenzug (mot)

ENGINEERS

FIELD ENGINEERS – HEADQUARTERS

Motorised Field Engineer
Regiment HQ
Stab eines Pionierregiments (mot)

HQ of a Part-motorised Field
Engineer Battalion
Stab eines Pionierbataillons (tmot)

Motorised HQ of a Field
Engineer Battalion
Stab eines Pionierbataillons (mot)

Panzer Engineer Battalion HQ
Stab eines Panzerpionierbataillons

HQ of a Part-motorised
Mountain Engineer Battalion
Stab eines Gebirgspionierbataillons (tmot)

HQ of a Part-motorised Field
Engineer Bridging Battalion
Stab eines Pionierbrückenbataillons (tmot)

Motorised HQ of a Bridging
Column Section
Stab eine Brückenkolonnenstaffel (mot)

Field Engineer Park
Battalion HQ
Stab eines Pionierparkbataillons

Commander of a Field Engineer
Company
Führer einer Pionierkompanie

FIELD ENGINEERS – UNITS

Field Engineer Company
Pionierkompanie

Mountain Engineer Company — *Gebirgspionierkompanie*

Motorised Field Engineer Company — *Pionierkompanie (mot)*

Motorised Light Field Engineer Company — *leichte Pionierkompanie (mot)*

Panzer Engineer Company — *Panzerpionierkompanie*

Field Engineer Company with Armoured Personal Carriers — *Pionierkompanie auf Schützenpanzerwagen*

Field Engineer Company on bicycles — *Pionierkompanie auf Fahrrädern*

Field Engineer Listening Platoon[5] — *Pionierhorchzug*

Field Engineer Assault Boat Section — *Pioniersturmbootkommando*

Field Engineer Landing Assault Boat Company — *Pionierlandungssturmboot-Kompanie*

Field Engineer Landing Boat Company — *Pionierlandungsbootkompanie*

Field Engineer Landing Ferry Company — *Pionierlandungsfähren-Kompanie*

---

5 Utilised loops of cable between the lines to pick up enemy field telephone conversations by induction. Up to 20 telephones could be listened into via one loop.

Field Engineer Vehicle Park Company — *Pionierparkkompanie*

Field Engineer Bridging Company — *Pionier-brückenkompanie*

Motorised Field Engineer Repairs Platoon — *Pioniermaschinezug (mot)*

Motorised Field Engineer Signals Platoon — *Nachrichtenzug (mot) der Pioniere*

Signals Platoon of a Part-motorised Mountain Engineer Platoon — *Nachrichtenzug eines Gebirgspionierbataillons (tmot)*

Light Field Engineer Column — *leichte Pionierkolonne*

Motorised Light Field Engineer Column — *leichte Pionierkolonne (mot)*

Small Field Engineer Column with Motor Vehicles — *kleine Pionierkraftwagenkolonne*

Motorised Light Mountain Engineer Column — *leichte Gebirgspionierkolonne (mot)*

Mountain Engineer Section with Hand Carts — *Gebirgspionierkarrenstaffel*

Motorised Bridging Column with Type 'B' Equipment (or Type 'C', 'K' etc. depending upon the letter used)[6]

Brückenkolonne (mot) B-Gerät (C-Gerät bzw., K-Gerät usw.)

Bridging Column with Type 'T' equipment

Brückenkolonne T-Gerät

Motorised Transport Column for Heavy Bridging Equipment

Transportkolonne für schweres Brückengerät (mot)

Prime Mover Section of a Bridging Column with Type 'B' Equipment (or other equipments, dependent upon signifying letter)

Kraftzugstaffel einer Brückenkolonne B (oder anderen Gerät)

Unit with Light Bridging Equipment, which can be dismantled

Einheit leichts zerlegbares Brückengerät

Unit with Light Bridging Equipment (able to be dismantled), with Escort

Einheit leichts zerlegbares Brückengerät mit Begleitkommando

Unit equipped with 'Herbert'-type Bridging Equipment

Einheit Herbertgerät

Unit equipped with 'Herbert'-type Bridging Equipment, with Escort

Einheit Herbertgerät mit Begleitkommando

Unit with 'B' type Bridging Column Equipment

Geräteinheit Brückenkolonne B

---

6 Guide to varieties of German bridging equipment with their official designations:

Type	Capacity in tons	Roadway
B	4.5–20	Single road
C	Up to 5.9	Single track
K	Up to 27	Box girder single road
T	4.5–10	Single road
Z	Up to 33	Single road
J42/J43	c. 30	Box girder span to 64 feet, with J43 having capacity for larger span
Z	Up to 33	Road

Unit with 'B' type Bridging
Column Equipment,
with Escort

*Geräteinheit Brückenkolonne B
mit Begleitkommando*

FIELD ENGINEERS – WEAPONS

Flamethrower   Y   *Flammenwerfer*

Heavy Flamethrower (Static)   *schwerer Flammenwerfer (ortsfest)*

FIELD ENGINEERS – ORGANISATION

Organisational example:
  Motorised Field Engineer
      Battalion with
          HQ
3 Motorised Field Engineer
  Companies, each with 2
  Heavy Machine-guns, 9
  Light Machine-guns, 3
Light Anti-tank Rifles, 2
      Heavy Mortars,
Motorised Light Engineer
  Column with 2 Light
      Machine-guns

*Pionierbataillon (mot) zu
1 Stab
3 Pionierkompanien (mot)
mit je 2 s M.G., 9 le M.G., 3
le Pz.B., 2 s GrW.,
1 le Pionierkolonne (mot) mit
2 le M.G.*

Examples of symbols as they would appear on maps:

29th Motorised Field
Engineer Battalion

Pionierbataillon 29 (mot)

March Column of Field
Engineer Units, arrow
indicating direction of
movement

*Marschkolonne von
Pioniereinheiten*

FORTRESS ENGINEERS – HEADQUARTERS

Fortress Engineer HQ *Festungspionierstab*

Fortress Engineer Sector Group *Festungspionierabschnittsgruppe*

Fortress Department *Festungsdienststelle*

Fortress Engineer Battalion HQ *Stab eines Festungspionierbataillons*

FORTRESS ENGINEERS – UNITS

Fortress Engineer Company *Festungspionierkompanie*

Technical Fortress Park Company *technische Festungsparkkompanie*

Rock Boring Company *Gesteinsbohrkompanie*

Fortress Engineer Park Company *Festungspionierparkkompanie*

Fortress Construction Company *Festungsbaustoffkolonne*

Military Geology Post *Wehrgeologenstelle*

Fortress Engineer Park ꜰ▢   *Festungspionierpark*

Fortress Engineer Park (within
Germany only) ꜰ▣   *Heimatfestungspionierpark*

FORTRESS ENGINEERS – ORGANISATION

Organisational example:

Fortress Engineer Battalion
with
1 HQ,
3 Fortress Engineer
Companies,
1 Technical Fortress
Vehicle Park Company

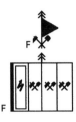

*Festungspionierbataillon zu
1 Stab
3 Festungspionierkompanie
1 technische
Festungsparkkompanie*

CONSTRUCTION / ROAD CONSTRUCTION ENGINEERS –
HEADQUARTERS

Engineer Regiment HQ z.b.V.   *Pionierregimentsstab z. b. V*

Construction Engineer
Battalion HQ   *Stab eines Baupionierbataillons*

Road Construction Engineer
Battalion HQ   *Stab eines
Straßenbaupionierbataillons*

HQ of a Light Road
Construction Engineer
Battalion on Bicycles   *Stab eines leichten
Straßenbaupionierbataillons auf
Fahrrädern*

Motorised Snow-clearing
Unit HQ   *Stab einer Schneeräumabteilung
(mot)*

CONSTRUCTION / ROAD CONSTRUCTION ENGINEERS – UNITS

Construction Engineer Company *Baupionierkompanie*

Motorised Construction Engineer Column *Baupionierkolonne (mot)*

Construction Engineer Column *Baupionierkolonne*

Mountain Construction Engineer Column *Gebirgsbaupionierkolonne*

Road Construction Engineer Company *Straßenbaupionierkompanie*

Part-motorised Road Construction Engineer Company *Straßenbaupionierkompanie (tmot)*

Light Road Construction Engineer Company on Bicycles *leichte Straßenbaupionierkompanie auf Fahrrädern*

Part-motorised Equipment Section of a Road Construction Engineer Battalion *Gerätestaffel (tmot) eines Straßenbaupionierbataillions*

Snow-clearing Company *Schneeräumkompanie*

Snow-blower Platoon *Schneefräsenzug*

Snow-blower Section *Schneefräsenhalbzug*

Snow-clearing Unit *Schneeräumtrupp*

SIGNALS AND COMMUNICATIONS TROOPS

SIGNALS AND COMMUNICATIONS TROOPS – HEADQUARTERS

Motorised Signals Battalion HQ (Headquarters = Fü, Army Group = HGr, Army = A, Corps = K, Division = D)		*Stab einer (Führungs = Fü, Heeresgruppen = HGr, Armee = A, Korps = K, Division = D) Nachrichtenabteilung (mot)*
Panzer Signals Battalion HQ (Army = A, Corps = K, Division = D)		*Stab einer Panzer (Armee = A, Korps = K, Divisions = D) Nachrichtenabteilung*
Part-motorised Mountain Signals Battalion HQ (Corps = K, Division = D)		*Stab einer Gebirgs (Korps = K, Divisions = D) Nachrichtenabteilung (tmot)*
Commander of a Signals Company		*Führer einer Nachrichtenkompanie*

SIGNALS AND COMMUNICATIONS TROOPS – UNITS

TERRITORIAL AND HEADQUARTERS SIGNALS UNITS

Signals Company		*Nachrichtenkompanie*
Part-motorised Signals Company		*Nachrichtenkompanie (tmot)*
Motorised Signals Company		*Nachrichtenkompanie (mot)*
Motorised Light Signals Column		*leichte Nachrichtenkolonne (mot)*

WWII GERMAN MILITARY SYMBOLS

TELEPHONE AND TELEPRINTER UNITS

Motorised Telephone Company *Fernsprechkompanie (mot)*

Part-motorised Mountain
Telephone Company *Gebirgsfernsprechkompanie (tmot)*

Panzer Telephone Company *Panzerfernsprechkompanie*

Part-motorised Field Telephone
Cable-laying Company *Feldfernkabelkompanie (mot)*

RADIO UNITS

Motorised Radio Company *Funkkompanie (mot)*

Panzer Radio Company *Panzerfunkkompanie*

Part-motorised Mountain
Radio Company *Gebirgsfunkkompanie (tmot)*

SIGNALS AND COMMUNICATIONS TROOPS –
SIGNALS COMMUNICATION SERVICES

TELEPHONE AND TELEPRINTER SERVICE TROOPS

Light Field Cable-laying Unit 3
(n.b.: 3 = unit possesses 3km of
telephone cable ; 6 = 6km of
telephone cable, etc. etc.) *Leichter Feldkabeltrupp 3*
(Anm: 3 = 3km f. Feldkabel)

Medium Field Cable-laying
Unit 6 (Horse-drawn)

*Mittlerer Feldkabeltrupp 6
(bespannt)*

Motorised Heavy Field
Cable-laying Unit 10

Schwerer Feldkabeltrupp 10 (mot)

Motorised Heavy Field
Cable-laying Unit 10 with
Half-tracks

*Schwerer Feldkabeltrupp 10 (mot)
auf Halbkette*

Heavy Armoured Field
Cable-laying Unit (Figure
corresponds to Cable
Length carried)

*Schwerer Feldkabeltrupp (gp)
(Anm: Zahl entspricht
Kabelausstattung)*

Part-motorised Signal
Cable-laying Unit

Feldfernkabeltrupp (tmot)

Motorised Light Telephone
Maintenance Unit

*Leichter
Fernsprechinstandhaltungstrupp
(mot)*

Motorised Telephone
Operating Unit

Fernsprechbetriebstrupp (mot)

POSTS AND POSITIONS

Telephone Office

Fernsprechstelle

Telephone Exchange /
Switchboard

Fernsprechvermittlung

Switchboard of a Divisional
Signals Battalion

*Vermittlung einer
Divisionsnachrichtenabteilung*

Switchboard of a Corps Signals
Battalion

*Vermittlung einer
Korpsnachrichtenabteilung*

Switchboard of an Army Signals Regiment (A) *Vermittlung einer Armeenachrichtenregiments*

Switchboard of an Army Group Signals Regiment (G) *Vermittlung einer Heeresgruppennachrichten-regiments*

Switchboard of a Railway Signals Unit (T) *Vermittlung einer Eisenbahnnachrichteneinheit*

Switchboard of other Army Signals Units (e.g. Field Signals Commander, etc.) (H) *Vermittlung sonstiger Nachrichteneinheiten des Heeres (Feldnachrichtenkommandantur usw.)*

Switchboard of a Signals Unit of the Supreme Command, Armed Forces (W) *Vermittlung von Nachrichteneinheiten des OKW*

Switchboard of a Luftwaffe Signals Unit (L) *Vermittlung von Nachrichteneinheiten der Luftwaffe*

Switchboard of a Navy Signals Unit (M) *Vermittlung von Nachrichteneinheiten der Kriegsmarine*

Garrison Switchboard (S) *Standortvermittlung*

Switchboard for a Static Position (O) *Ortsvermittlung*

CABLES

Single Field Cable ——— *Feldkabeleinfachleitung*

Double Field Cable +——+ *Feldkabeldoppeleinfachleitung*

Long-distance Cable ╼╫─╫╾ *Feldfernkabel*

OVERHEAD LINES

Armed Forces Overhead Lines (for the Post or Railways)	•—•—•	*Blankdrahtlinie der Wehrmacht (= Freileitungslinie der Post oder Bahn usw.)*

SIGNALS AND COMMUNICATIONS TROOPS – RADIO COMMUNICATIONS SERVICE

TROOPS

Portable Radio Unit (Short Wave Radio)		*Tornisterfunktrupp b Kzw (Anm.: Kzw = Kurzwelle)*
Mounted Portable Radio Unit (Short Wave Radio)		*Tornisterfunktrupp b Kzw (beritten)*
Motorised Portable Radio Unit (Ultra-Short Wave Radio)		*Tornisterfunktrupp b UKw (mot) (Anm.: UKw = Ultrakurzwelle)*
Portable Radio Unit (Medium Wave Radio)		*Tornisterfunktrupp g Mw*
Motorised Light Radio Unit (5 Mw Radio, approx 5km range)[7]		*Leichter Funktrupp 5 Mw (mot)*
Motorised Aviation Radio Unit (20 Ultra-Short Wave Radio, approx 20km range)		*Leichter Fliegerfunktrupp 20 UKw (mot)*
Horse-drawn Medium Radio Unit (5 Mw Radio, approx 5km range)		*Mittlerer Funktrupp 5 Mw (bespannt) (Anm: Mw = Mittelwelle)*

---

7   The radio ranges noted are only approximate.

Armoured Light Radio Unit (80 Mw Radio) *Leichter Funktrupp 80 Mw (gp)*

Armoured Medium Radio Unit (15 Short Wave Radio, approx 15km range), as yet still not equipped with Armoured Cars *Mittlerer Funktrupp 15 Kzw (gp), soweit noch nicht mit s.Pz.-Spähwagen ausgeststtet*

Armoured Command Radio Unit (Note: the numbers correspond to the Radio Equipment in use) *Kommando Funktrupp (gp), (Kdo. Fu. Tr. Gp) (Anm: Zahlen entsprechend Geräteausstattung einsetzen)*

Command Panzer *Panzerbefehlswagen*

Motorised Cipher Unit *Schlüsseltrupp (mot)*

POSTS AND POSITIONS

Radio Station *Funkstelle*

Transmitter // *Sender*

Receiver // *Empfänger*

CONNECTIONS

Utilised by a number of units, incl. Police, SS, Gestapo,
as well as main branches of the Armed Forces

Radio Net (Line)[8]   *Linie*

Radio Net (Double Line)[9]   *Doppellinie*

Radio Net ('Star')[10]   *Stern*

Radio Net ('Area')[11]   *Kreis*

8 One station to a single other station, no command set.
9 One command station to two subordinate sub-stations.
10 One command station to three or more subordinate sub-stations.
11 A number of independent stations in contact with each other; no command station.

OTHER UNITS AND CONNECTIONS

Signal Lamp Unit   ⍺   *Blinktrupp*

Signal Lamp Line   ⍺--⍥   *Blinklinie*

Heliograph Signals Units   ⌠   *Lichtsprechtrupp*

Line of Sight for Heliographs   ⌠------⌐   *Lichtsprechlinie*

Message Dog Pack   ⋋⋌   *Meldehundrotte*

Pigeon Loft   ▭   *Brieftaubenschlag*

Reporting Centre   MKpf   *Meldekopf*

Report Collection Centre   Ⓜ   *Meldesammelstelle*

SIGNALS AND COMMUNICATIONS TROOPS – USE OF COLOUR
WITHIN SIGNALS AND COMMUNICATIONS DOCUMENTS

In sketches and plans illustrating means of communication, units, lines, etc., different colours are used to denote ownership of the communication nets. These are as follows:

Green	Armed Forces Supreme Command, Army High Command, Signals units (except for Artillery)
Red	Army Supreme Command, Artillery
Blue	Luftwaffe, Army Corps
Black	Navy
Brown	Army Group, Division
Violet	Railways
Orange	Post

RAILWAY TROOPS

RAILWAY TROOPS – HEADQUARTERS

Motorised Railway Engineer
Battalion HQ

*Stab eines
Eisenbahnpionierbataillons (Mot)*

RAILWAY TROOPS – UNITS

Motorised Railway
Engineer Company

Eisenbahnpionierkompanie (Mot)

RAILWAY OPERATING TROOPS – UNITS

Field Railway Operating
Company

Feldeisenbahnbetriebskompanie

FIELD WATERWAY UNITS

Inland Waterway
Minesweeping Section

Feldwasserstraßenräumzug

TECHNICAL TROOPS

TECHNICAL TROOPS – HEADQUARTERS

Motorised Technical Battalion HQ *Stab eines Technischen Bataillons (mot)*

TECHNICAL TROOPS – UNITS

Motorised Technical Company *Technische Kompanie (mot)*

PROPAGANDA UNITS

Motorised Propaganda Company *Propagandakompanie (mot)*

PART IV

SUPPLY AND REAR-AREA TROOPS

BAGGAGE TRAIN UNITS

Motorised Rations Train ⊠ᵥ *Verpflegungstroß (mot)*

Rations Train Type I ⊠ᵥᵢ *Verpflegungstroß I*

Rations Train Type II ⊠ᵥᵢᵢ *Verpflegungstroß II*

Motorised Rations Train Type II ⊠ᵥᵢᵢ *Verpflegungstroß II (mot)*

Baggage Train ⊠Gep *Gepäcktroß*

Motorised Baggage Train ⊠Gep *Gepäcktroß (mot)*

Battle Baggage Train[1] ⊠Gef *Gefechtstroß*

Motorised Battle Baggage Train ⊠Gef *Gefechtstroß (mot)*

---

1 Those echelons that followed immediately behind the initial line of advancing troops, i.e. a Reconnaissance Battalion's repairs column. They carried items such as ammunition, rations, water, medical supplies, etc.

77

Examples showing baggage trains with particular arms-of-service:

Battle Train of a Field Engineer Battalion	⊠	*Gefechtstroß eines* *Pionierbataillons*
Battle Train of a Panzer Battalion	⊠	*Gefechtstroß eines* *Panzerabteilung*
Battle Train of an Artillery Battalion	⊠	*Gefechtstroß eines* *Artillerieabteilung*

SUPPLY TROOPS

Colours used to distinguish different types of supply troops:

Railways	**Violet**
Munitions/Ordnance	**Blue**
Supply	**Brown**
Administration units	**Green**
Medical units	**Light Red**
Veterinary units	**Carmine Red**
Motor vehicle park units	**Pink**
Field Post	**Yellow**

SUPPLY TROOPS – HEADQUARTERS

Motor Transport Regiment HQ		*Stab eines* *Kraftwagentransportregiments*
Commander of Motorised Corps Supply Troops HQ		*Stab eines Kommandeurs der* *Korpsnachschubtruppen (mot)*
Commander of a Panzer Corps Supply Troops HQ		*Stab eines Kommandeurs der* *Panzerkorpsnachschubtruppen*

Commander of Motorised
Divisional Supply Troops HQ

*Stab eines Kommandeurs der
Divisionsnachschubtruppen (mot)*

Commander of Panzer
Divisional Supply Troops HQ

*Stab eines Kommandeurs der
Panzerdivisionsnachschubtruppen*

Motor Transport Battalion HQ
(Goods Transport)

*Stab einer
Kraftwagentransportabteilung*

Motorised Transport Battalion
HQ (Personnel Transport)

Stab einer Kraftfahrabteilung

Supply Train Battalion HQ

Stab einer Fahrabteilung

Mountain Supply
Column Unit HQ

*Stab einer
Gebirgsnachschubkolonnen-
abteilung*

Motorised Supply Battalion HQ

*Stab eines Nachschubbataillons
(mot)*

Supply Battalion HQ

Stab eines Nachschubbataillons

Motorised Mountain
Supply Battalion HQ

*Stab einer
Gebirgsnachschubbataillons (mot)*

Mountain Transport
Battalion HQ

Stab einer Gebirgsträgerbataillons

Transloading /
Transshipment HQ[2]

Umschlagstab

Commander of Motor
Transport Company or a Motor
Transport Column

*Führer einer
Kraftwagentransportkompanie
und Kraftwagentransportkolonne*

2   For instance, when transferring between road and rail, ship and rail, etc.

SUPPLY TROOPS – UNITS

Motor Transport Company
equipped with Trucks
*Kraftwagentransportkompanie
(Lkw.)*

Supply Squadron (60t capacity)
Fahrschwadron (60t)

Motorised Transport Company
Kraftfahrkompanie

Section of a Motorised
Transport Company
Zug einer Kraftfahrkompanie

Supply Company
Nachschubkompanie

Motorised Supply Company
Nachschubkompanie (mot)

Mountain Supply Company
Gebirgsnachschubkompanie

Mountain Transport Company
Gebirgsträgerkompanie

Large Motor Vehicle Column
(60t capacity)
Große Kraftwagenkolonne (60 t)

Small Motor Vehicle Column
(30t capacity)
Kleine Kraftwagenkolonne (30 t)

Large Supply Column (60t
capacity) of a Horse-drawn
Supply Column Unit
*Große Fahrkolonne (60 t) einer
Nachschubkolonnenabteilung
(besp.)*

Small Supply Column (30t capacity) — *Kleine Fahrkolonne (30 t)*

Light Supply Column (15t capacity) *le* — *Leichte Fahrkolonne (15 t)*

Mountain Motor Vehicle Column (30t capacity) *Gebirgskraftwagenkolonne (30 t)*

Mountain Supply Column *Gebirgsfahrkolonne*

Mountain Column with Two-wheeled Carts (10t capacity) *Kar* *Gebirgskarrenkolonne (10 t)*

Mule Column (10t capacity) —ᵀ *Tragtierkolonne (10 t)*

Small Motor Transport Column for transporting Fuel (25 cubic metre capacity) *Kleine Kraftwagenkolonne für Betriebsstoff (25 cbm)*

Large Motor Transport Column for transporting Fuel (50 cubic metre capacity) *Große Kraftwagenkolonne für Betriebsstoff (50 cbm)*

Tanker Wagon Column (via road or rail) *Kes* *Kesselwagenkolonne*

Bus Column *Kom* *Kraftomnibuskolonne*

SUPPLY TROOPS – FACILITIES

Central / Main Ammunition Depot   [M]ʜ   *Heeresmunitionslager*

Army-level Ammunition Depot   [M]ᴀ   *Armeemunitionslager*

Corps Ammunition Depot   [M]ᴋ   *Korpsmunitionslager*

Ammunition Distribution Point   [M]   *Munitionsausgabestelle*

Ammunition Supply Point   [M]   *Munitionsumschlagstelle*

Central Fuel and Bulk Lubricant Storage Depot   [BetrSt]ʜ   *Heeresbetriebsstofflager*

Army-level Fuel and Bulk Lubricant Storage Depot   [BetrSt]ᴀ   *Armeebetriebsstofflager*

Corps Fuel and Bulk Lubricant Storage Depot   [BetrSt]ᴋ   *Korpsbetriebsstofflager*

Distribution Position for Fuel   *Ausgabestelle für Betriebsstoff*

Fuel Filling Station for Individual Vehicles   *Tankstelle für Einzelfahrzeuge*

Fuel and Lubrication Railhead, Bulk Reduction Point ('Full')   *Eisenbahntankstelle (gefüllt)*

Permanent Fuel Filling Station   *Ortsfeste Tankstelle*

MOTOR TRANSPORT TROOPS

MOTOR TRANSPORT TROOPS – UNITS

Motorised Workshop Company   *Werkstattkompanie (mot)*

Panzer Workshop Company   *Pz-Werkstattkompanie*

Motor Vehicle
Workshop Platoon   *Kw. Werkstattzug*

Armoured Car
Workshop Platoon   *Pz–Spähwagen-Werkstattzug*

Motor Vehicle Repair Company   *Kfz-Instandsetzungskompanie*

Panzer Recovery Company   *Pz-Bergekompanie*

Panzer Recovery Platoon   *Pz-Bergezug*

Motor Vehicle
Recovery Platoon   *Kfz-Abschleppzug*

Motor Vehicle
Spare Parts Column   *Kfz-Ersatzteilkolonne*

Motor Vehicle
Spare Parts Section   *Kfz-Ersatzteilstaffel*

MOTOR TRANSPORT TROOPS – FACILITIES

Army Vehicle Park   *Armeekraftfahrpark*

Vehicle Park   *Kraftfahrpark*

RAILWAY TRANSPORTATION AND RAILWAY TRANSPORTATION FACILITIES

Ammunition Train   *Munitionszug*

Fuel Train   *Betriebsstoffzug*

Rations Supply Train   *Verpflegungszug*

Train transporting Construction Materials   *Baustoffzug*

Stationary Troop Transport Train   *Truppentransportzug (haltend)*

Troop Transport Train in Motion   *Truppentransportzug (in Fahrt)*

Stationary Empty Train   *Leerzug (haltend)*

Empty Train in Motion   *Leerzug (in Fahrt)*

WATER-SUPPLY UNITS

Heavy Motor Transport Column for Transporting Water (60 cubic metre capacity)   *Große Kraftwagenkolonne für Wasser 60cbm*

REAR-AREA SUPPLY UNITS AND DEPOTS

REAR-AREA SUPPLY UNITS AND DEPOTS – UNITS

Motorised Army Rations Depot   [AVA]   *Armeeverpflegungsamt (mot)*

Motorised Administration Company   [V]   *Verwaltungskompanie (mot)*

Bakery Company   [∅]   *Bäckereikompanie*

Motorised Butchery Company   [⊿]   *Schlächtereikompanie (mot)*

Motorised Army Clothing Depot   [ABA]   *Armeebekleidungsamt (mot)*

Army Billets Administration   [HUV]   *Heeresunterkunftsverwaltung*

REAR-AREA SUPPLY UNITS AND DEPOTS – FACILITIES

Army Rations Magazine   [HVM]   *Heeresverpflegungsmagazin*

Army Rations Depot   [AVL]   *Armeeverpflegungslager*

Corps Rations Depot   [KVL]   *Korpsverpflegungslager*

Divisional Rations Depot   [DVL]   *Divisionsverpflegungslager*

Ration Distribution Point   [V̂]   *Verpflegungsausgabestelle*

Rations Transhipping Station   ⊡   *Verpflegungsumschlagstelle*

Army Clothing Depot   [ABL]   *Armeebekleidungslager*

MEDICAL TROOPS

MEDICAL TROOPS – UNITS

Medical Company   ⊓   *Sanitätskompanie*

Motorised Medical Company   ⊓   *Sanitätskompanie (mot)*

Part-motorised Mountain Medical Company   ⊓   *Gebirgssanitätskompanie (tmot)*

Motorised Decontamination Company   [Eg]   *Truppenentgiftungskompanie (mot)*

Motorised Ambulance Company   [≡]   *Krankenkraftwagenkompanie*

Motorised Ambulance Platoon   ⊟   *Krankenkraftwagenzug*

Base Hospital   [K]   *Kriegslazarett*

Reserve Base Hospital   [RK]   *Reserve-Kriegslazarett*

Motorised Base Hospital   [K]   *Kriegslazarett (mot)*

Surgical Field Hospital   [F]   *Feldlazarett*

Motorised Surgical
Field Hospital   *Feldlazarett (mot)*

Medical Materials
Distribution Point   *Sanitätsmaterialausgabestelle*

Hospital Train   *Lazarettzug*

Emergency / Auxiliary
Casualty-Evacuation Train   *Behelfsmäßiger Verwundetenzug*

Disinfecting Train   *Entseuchungszug*

Hospital Ship   *Lazarettschiff*

MEDICAL TROOPS – FACILITIES SET-UP
ON THE MARCH AND IN BILLETS

Casualty Collection Station   *Krankensammelpunkt*

Medical Supplies Point   *Arztlicher Versorgungspunkt*

Casualty Collection Station of
an Ambulance Unit   *Krankensammelstelle einer
Krankentransportabteilung*

Area Surgical Centre (Non-
residential Patients)   *Ortskrankenstube*

Area Hospital (Non-residential
Patients)   *Ortslazarett*

MEDICAL TROOPS – BATTLEFIELD FACILITIES

First Aid Station   ⚕   *Verwundetennest*

Dressing Station   🅣   *Truppenverbandplatz*

Ambulance Loading Point   ⊗   *Wagenhalteplatz*

Main Casualty Clearing Station   △   *Hauptverbandplatz*

Collection Station for Walking Wounded   ♂   *Leichtverwundetensammelplatz*

Decontamination Centre (established by Decontamination Company)   [Eg]   *Truppen-Entgiftungsplatz (von Tr. Entg. Kp. eingerichtet)*

MEDICAL TROOPS – OTHER FACILITIES

Base Hospital (Residential Patients)   [K]   *Kriegslazarett (einges.)*

General Hospital (Residential Patients)   [R]   *Reservelazarett (einges.)*

General Base Hospital (Residential Patients)   [RK]   *Reservekriegslazarett (einges.)*

VETERINARY TROOPS

VETERINARY TROOPS – UNITS

Veterinary Company   *Veterinärkompanie*

Mountain Veterinary Company   *Gebirgsveterinärkompanie*

Army Horse Hospital   *Armeepferdelazarett*

Army Remount Depot   *Armeepferdepark*

Veterinary Research Station   *Veterinäruntersuchungsstelle*

Company for Transporting Horses   *Pferdetransportkompanie*

Motorised Company for Transporting Horses   *Pferdetransportkompanie (mot)*

VETERINARY TROOPS – FACILITIES

Dressing Station for Wounded Horses   *Pferdeverbandsplatz*

Collection Point for Wounded Horses   *Pferdesammelplatz*

ORDNANCE UNITS

Army Ordnance Park   ⬜A   *Armeegerätpark*

Arms Workshop   🔲   *Waffenwerkstatt*

Field Workshop   🔲Feld   *Feldwerkstatt*

MILITARY POLICE UNITS

Motorised Military
Police Company   🔲   *Feldgendarmeriekompanie (mot)*

Motorised Military Police Unit   ⟋   *Feldgendarmerietrupp (mot)*

FIELD POST OFFICE UNITS

Field Post Office   🔲   *Feldpostamt*

PART V

UNITS AND DEPARTMENTS WITH SPECIAL ASSIGNMENTS

ADMINISTRATIVE UNITS AND ASSIGNMENTS

ADMINISTRATIVE UNITS AND ASSIGNMENTS – HEADQUARTERS

Garrison Headquarters		*Standortkommandantur*
Garrison Headquarters for Large and Medium Cities (Military Government)		*Ortskommandantur I*
Garrison Headquarters for Small Cities, Towns and Villages (Military Government)		*Ortskommandantur II*

ADMINISTRATIVE UNITS AND ASSIGNMENTS – FACILITIES AND UNITS

Secret Field Police	GFP	*Geheime Feldpolizei*
Prisoner-of-War Camp (for Other Ranks)	Kgf Stalag	*Kgf-Mannschaftsstammlager*
Army-level Collection Point for Prisoners-of-War	Kgf A	*Armee-Kgf- Sammelstelle*
Counter-intelligence Unit	A	*Abwehrtrupp*

TRANSPORTATION DEPARTMENTS

Transport Control Headquarters | Trsp Kdtr | *Transportkommandantur*

Transport Liaison Point | Trsp Verb St | *Transportverbindungsstelle*

Railway Station Commander Grade I[1] | Bhf Kdtr I | *Bahnhofskommandantur I*

Railway Station Commander Grade II | Bhf Kdtr II | *Bahnhofskommandantur II*

Forwarding Station | W Ltg St | *Weiterleitungsstelle*

REAR-AREA CARE FACILITIES

Rest and Recreation Site (Operated by German Red Cross) | DRK | *Betreuungs und Verpflegungsstelle (betrieben durch DRK)*

Rest and Recreation Site (Operated by NSDAP Welfare Organisation) | NSV | *Betreuungs und Verpflegungsstelle (betrieben durch NSV)*

Delousing Station | EL | *Entlausungsanstalt*

Soldiers' Rest Home | S | *Soldatenheim*

---

1 Grades I or II depended upon whether the station accepted personnel *and* goods, or only goods, respectively.

Officers' Rest Home   🔲0   *Offiziersheim*

Army Rest Area   🔲W   *Wehrmachtaufenthaltsraum*

Army Billets   🔲U   *Wehrmachtunterkunft*

German Red Cross Aid Station   ⊕   *DRK – Hilfsstelle*

BORDER UNITS, PATROLS ETC.

Army Patrol
(Sergeant in Command)   ◆   *Heeresstreife (Feldwebelstreife)*

Army Patrol
(Officer in Command)   ◆   *Heeresstreife (Offiziersstreife)*

Railway Station Guard
Commander   ◉   *Bahnhofswachoffizier*

Railway Station Guard   ◉   *Bahnhofswache*

Border Guard Company   Gr🔲   *Grenzwachkompanie*

Border Post and Border Guards   Gr◆   *Grenzposten und Grenzwachen*

Leave Collection Company[3]   *Urlaubersammelkompanie*

Transportation Commander
and Train Guard (Officer)   *Transportführer und Zugwache
(Offizier)*

PENAL UNITS

Field Punishment Company   *Feldstrafgefangenenkompanie*

Field Punishment
Camp Company   *Feldstraflagerkompanie*

Field Disciplinary Company   *Feldsonderkompanie*

3 Troops returning from leave were collected in the Army or Corps rear area, and then despatched to the area they were needed. Up until 1943 troops returned direct to their parent units – officers continued to be allowed to do so until the end of the war.

PART VI

ABBREVIATIONS

English	Abbreviation	German
	A	
Reconnaissance Battalion	**A.A.**	*Aufklärungsabteilung*
Sector	**Abschn.**	*Abschnitt*
Battalion / Detachment / Unit	**Abt.**	*Abteilung*
Battalion / Detachment / Unit Commander	**Abt.Kdr.**	*Abteilungskommandeur*
Chief of National Defence (Supreme Command, Armed Forces)	**Abt.L.**	*Abteilung Landesverteidigung (im OKW)*
Battalion / Detachment / Unit Commander	**Abt.L.**	*Abteilungsleiter*
Transportation	**Abtrsp.**	*Abtransport*
Counter-intelligence / Defence	**Abw.**	*Abwehr*
Retired	**a.D.**	*Außer Dienst*
Army General Office[1]	**AHA**	*Allgemeines Heeresamt*
Army Headquarters	**AHQu**	*Armeehauptquartier*
Army Corps	**AK**	*Armeekorps*
Serving Officer	**akt.Offz.**	*aktiver Offizier*
Albanian	**alb.**	*albanisch*
Artillery Training Regiment	**ALR**	*Artillerie-Lehr-Regiment*
American	**amerik.**	*amerikanisch*
Army High Command	**AOK**	*Armeeoberkommando*
Army Postmaster	**APM**	*Armeepostmeister*
Artillery Regiment	**AR**	*Artillerie-Regiment*
Arado [aircraft company]	**Ar**	*Arado-Flugzeugbau*

1 Similar in function to AWA.

Arabian	**arab.**	*arabisch*
Artillery Commander	**Arko**	*Artilleriekommandeur*
Artillery Regiment	**Art.Rgt.**	*Artillerie-Regiment*
Army Detachment	**Arm.Abt.**	*Armee-Abteilung*
Army Group	**Armeegr.**	*Armeegruppe*
Admiral's Flag Officer[2]	**Asto.**	*Admiralstabsoffizier*
Reconnaissance	**Aufkl.**	*Aufklärung*
Training	**Ausb.**	*Ausbildung*
Training Regiment	**Ausb.Rgt.**	*Ausbildings-Regiment*
Artillery Liaison Command	**AVKO**	*Artillerieverbindungs-kommando*
Armed Forces General Office[3]	**AWA**	*Allgemeines Wehrmachtsamt*
Section for General Armed Forces Matters	**AWA**	*Amtsgruppe Allgemeine Wehrmachtangelegen-heiten*

B

Battery	**Battr.**	*Batterie*
Commander of the Army Reserve	**BdE**	*Befehlshaber des Ersatzheeres*
Fortification	**Befest.**	*Befestigung*
Commander	**Befh.**	*Befehlshaber*
Commander of an Army's Rear Area	**Bef.r.H.G.**	*Befehlshaber rückwärtiges Heeresgebiet*
Escort Battalion	**Begl.Btl.**	*Begleit-Bataillon*
on either side of... / mutually	**beiders.**	*beiderseits*
Belgium	**belg.**	*belgisch*
Observation Battalion / Det.	**Beob.Abt.**	*Beobachtungs-Abteilung*
Area / Sector	**Ber.**	*Bereich*
Horse-drawn	**besp.**	*bespannt*
Operating Battalion[4]	**Betr.Abt.**	*Betriebs-Abteilung*

2 Essentially an Admiral's aide-de-camp.
3 Controlled various branches, e.g. welfare, pensions, and other personnel matters, PoWs, Military Science, etc.
4 Usually referring to operating railways, transport, etc.

Authorised agent / Plenipotentiary	**Bev.**	*Bevollmächtigter*
General possessing plenipotentiary powers, i.e. control over both military and civilian elements within his command area	**Bev.Gen.**	*Bevollmächtigter General*
Mobile	**bewegl. / bwgl.**	*beweglich*
Bavarian Aircraft Co. (Messerschmitt)	**Bf**	*Bayerische Flugzeugwerke*
Motorcycle w/sidecar	**B-Krad**	*Beiwagenkraftrad*
Static	**bodst. / bo.**	*bodenständig*
Ship-based Aircraft	**Bordfl. / B.Fl.**	*Bordflieger*
'Brandenburg' units	**BR**	*Brandenburg-Verbände*
Brigade	**Brig.**	*Brigade*
SS Major-General	**Brig.Fhr.**	*SS-Brigadeführer*
British	**brit.**	*britisch*
Registered Tonnage	**BRT**	*Brutto-Register-tonne*
Bridging Column	**Brüko.**	*Brückenkolonne*
Observation Post / Position	**B-Stelle**	*Beobachtungsstelle*
Battalion	**Btl.**	*Bataillon*
Battery	**Bttr.**	*Batterie*
Bücker [aircraft co.]	**Bü.**	*Bücker*
Bulgarian	**bulg.**	*bulgarisch*
Blohm und Voss [aircraft co.]	**Bv**	*Blohm und Voss*

C

C-in-C, General Staff	**Chef d. Gen.St.**	*Chef des Generalstabes*
C-in-C, Army Equipment, and Commander of the Reserve	**Chef H Rü u.BdE**	*Chef der Heeresrüstung und Befehlshaber des Ersatzheeres*

D

German Labour Organisation[5]	**DAF**	*Deutsche Arbeitsfront*
German Afrika Korps	**DAK**	*Deutsches Afrikakorps*
SS-Panzergrenadier-Regiment 4 "Der Führer"	**DF**	*4th SS Panzergrenadier Rgt. "Der Führer"*
German Research Institute for Gliders[6]	**DFS**	*Deutsches Forschungs-institut für Segelflug*
German Army Mission	**DHM**	*Deutsche Heeresmission*
Divisional Supply Commander	**Dinafü.**	*Divisions-Nachschubführer*
Division	**Div.**	*Division*
Divisional Fusilier Battalion	**Div.Füs.Btl.**	*Divisions-Füsilier-Bataillon*
Divisional Group	**Div.Grp.**	*Divisions-Gruppe*
Divisional Signals Battalion	**Div.Nachr.Abt.**	*Divisions-Nachrichten-Abteilung*
Divisional HQ	**Div.Stab.**	*Divisions-Stab*
Dornier [aircraft co.]	**Do**	*Dornier*
German	**dt.**	*deutsch*
of the Reserve[7]	**d.R.**	*der Reserve*
German Railways	**DR**	*Deutsche Reichsbahn*
German Red Cross	**DRK**	*Deutsches Rotes Kreuz*
German Postal Service	**DRP**	*Deutsche Reichspost*
German Liaison Command[8]	**DVK**	*Deutsches Verbindungskommando*
German commercial flying school	**DVS**	*Deutsche Verkehrsfliegerschule*

5 A NSDAP civilian organisation.
6 Manufactured gliders.
7 An officer noted as 'd.R.' was normally attached to the Wehrkreis reserve HQ of corps and divisions.
8 At national-level.

E

Unit	**Einh.**	*Einheit*
Action / Combat / Operation	**Eins.**	*Einsatz*
Railway	**Eisb.**	*Eisenbahn*
Iron Cross	**EK**	*Eisernes Kreuz*
Oak Leaf[9]	**El**	*Eichenlaub*
Ground Combat	**Erdkpf.**	*Erdkampf*
Replacement Regiment	**Erg.Rgt.**	*Ergänzungs-Regiment*
Reconnaissance	**Erk.**	*Erkundung*
Reserve Company / Battalion, etc.	**Ers.Kp. / Btl.**	*Ersatz-Kompanie / Bataillon, usw.*
Squadron	**Esk.**	*Eskadron*
Estonian	**est.**	*estnisch*
Test Centre	**E-Stelle**	*Erprobungstselle*
Railway Transport	**E-Transp.**	*Eisenbahn-Transport*

F

Long-range Reconnaissance	**(F)**	*Fernaufklärung (Luftwaffe)*
Field Artillery	**Fa.**	*Feldartillerie*
Field Training Battalion	**FAA**	*Feld-Ausbildungs-Abteilung*
Anti-aircraft Artillery School	**FAS**	*Flakartillerieschule*
Führer Escort Division	**FBD**	*Führer-Begleit-Division*
Führer Escort Battalion	**F.Bgl.btl.**	*Führer-Begleit-Bataillon*
Airfield Operating Company	**FBK**	*Flughafenbetriebs-kompanie*
Enemy	**Fd./fdl.**	*feindlich*
Commander of Minesweepers	**F.d.M.**	*Führer der Minensuchboote*
Commander of MTBs	**F.d.S.**	*Führer der Schnellboote*
Commander of Destroyers	**F.d.Z.**	*Führer der Zerstörer*

9 As in 'Knight's Cross with Oak Leaves'.

Field Reserve Battalion	**FEB**	*Feldersatz-Bataillon*
Field Training	**Feldausb. (FAD)**	*Feldausbildung*
Field Reserve / Replacement	**Felders.**	*Feldersatz*
Military Police	**Feldgend.**	*Feldgendarmerie*
Fortress Battalion / Regiment, etc.	**Fest.Btl. / Rgt.**	*Festungs-Bataillon / Regiment, usw.*
Fortress	**Festg.**	*Festung*
Fortress HQ	**Fest.Stab**	*Festungsstab*
Führer Grenadier Division	**FGD**	*Führer-Grenadier-Division*
Volunteer Grenadier Regiment	**FGR**	*Freiwilligen-Grenadier-Regiment*
Field Howitzer	**FH**	*Feldhaubitze*
Main Operations Office	**FHA**	*Führungshauptamt*
'Feldherrnhalle' units	**FHH**	*Feldherrnhalle*
Führer Headquarters	**FHQu.**	*Führerhauptquartier*
Senior Officer Candidate	**Fhr.**	*Fähnrich*
Fieseler [aircraft company]	**Fi**	*Fieseler*
Finnish	**finn.**	*finnisch*
Officer Candidate	**Fj., Fhj.**	*Fahnenjunker*
Parachute Division	**FJD**	*Fallschirmjägerdivision*
Parachute Regiment	**FJR**	*Fallschirmjäger-Regiment*
Anti-aircraft Artillery	**Flak**	*Flieger-Abwehrkanone*
Anti-aircraft Artillery Company / Battalion, etc.	**Fla.Kp. / Btl.**	*Fliegerabwehr-Kompanie / Bataillon, usw.*
Field Hospital	**F-Laz.**	*Feldlazarett*
Ground Defence Area within a Luftgau	**FLg.**	*Feldluftgau*
Comanders, Luftwaffe Fighters	**Fliefü**	*Fliegerführer*
Pilot / Airman	**Flieg. / Flg.**	*Flieger*
Air Liaison Officer	**Flivo**	*Fliegerverbindungsoffizier*
Air Corps	**Fl.K. / Flg.K.**	*Fliegerkorps*
Flotilla	**Flott.**	*Flotille*

Fokker [aircraft company]	**Fo**	*Fokker*
Field Post Office	**FPA**	*Feldpostamt*
Field Post Survey	**FpÜ.**	*Feldpost-Übersicht*
Fusilier Regiment	**FR**	*Füsilier-Regiment*
French	**franz. / frz.**	*französisch*
Frigate (Frigate's Captain / Commander)	**Freg. (Freg.Kpt.)**	*Fregatte (Fregattenkapitän)*
Volunteer	**Freiw. / Frw.**	*Freiwillige*
Parachute	**Fsch.**	*Fallschirm*
Parachute Division	**Fs.Jg.Div.**	*Fallschirm-Jäger-Division*
Telephone	**Fspr.**	*Fernsprech*
Peacetime Garrison	**FstO.**	*Friedensstandort*
Fusilier	**Füs.**	*Füsilier*
Focke-Wulf [aircraft company]	**Fw**	*Focke-Wulf*
Sergeant	**Fw.**	*Feldwebel*
Munitions / Ordnance Battalion	**Fz.Btl.**	*Feldzeug-Bataillon*

G

Galician	**gal. / galiz.**	*galizisch*
'Grossdeutschland' units	**GD**	*Großdeutschland*
Mountain Division	**Geb.Div.**	*Gebirgs-Division*
Mountain Infantry Regiment	**Geb.Jg.Rgt.**	*Gebirgsjäger-Regiment*
Lance-Corporal	**Gefr.**	*Gefreiter*
Command Post	**Gef.Std.**	*Gefechtsstand*
Secret	**geh.**	*geheim*
Suitable for cross-country use	**gel. / gl.**	*geländegängig*
Mixed / Composite	**gem.**	*gemischt*
General of Artillery	**Gen.d.Art.**	*General der Artillerie*

Field Marshal	**Gen.Feldm.**	*Generalfeldmarschall*
Corps Command	**Gen.Kdo.**	*Generalkommando*
Lieutenant-General	**Gen.Lt.**	*Generalleutnant*
Major-General	**Gen.Maj.**	*Generalmajor*
General	**Gen.Oberst**	*Generaloberst*
Quartermaster-General	**Gen.Qu.**	*Generalquartiermeister*
Armoured	**gep.**	*gepanzert*
Germanic	**germ.**	*germanisch*
Gun	**Gesch.**	*Geschütz*
Field Marshal	**GFM**	*Generalfeldmarschall*
General Government	**GG**	*Generalgouvernement*
Mountain Infantry Regiment	**GJR**	*Gebirgsjäger Regiment*
Corps Command	**GKdo.**	*Generalkommando*
Secret command information[10]	**g.Kdos.**	*geheime Kommandosache*
Major-General	**Gm.**	*Generalmajor*
Gotha [aircraft company]	**Go**	*Gothaer Waggonfabrik-flugzeugwerke*
Grenadier Regiment	**GR**	*Grenadierregiment*
Mortar	**Gra.We. / Gr.W.**	*Granatwerfer*
Grenadier	**Gren.**	*Grenadier*
Group Command	**Gr.Kdo.**	*Gruppenkommando*
SS Lieutenant-General	**Gruf.**	*SS-Gruppenführer*
Border Regiment	**Grz.Rgt.**	*Grenz-Regiment*

10 i.e., information for disclosure to the commander of recipient unit.

H

Army	**H.**	*Heer*
Senior Artillery Commander with an Army Group	**HARKo**	*Höherer Artilleriekommandeur bei Heeresgruppe*
Army Artillery	**H.Art.**	*Heeres-Artillerie*
Heinkel [aircraft company]	**He**	*Heinkel-Flugzeugbau*
lit. Homeland, but might be used to refer to a unit based in Germany	**Heim.**	*Heimat*
Army Anti-aircraft Artillery	**H.Flakart.**	*Heeres-Flakartillerie*
Senior Sergeant	**Hfw.**	*Hauptfeldwebel*
'Hermann Göring' units	**HG**	*Hermann Göring*
Army Group	**HGr.**	*Heeresgruppe*
Auxiliary	**HiWi**	*Hilfswilliger*
Auxiliary Cruiser	**HK**	*Hilfskreuzer*
Senior Command	**H.Kdo.**	*Höheres Kommando*
Main Battle Zone	**HKF**	*Hauptkampffeld*
Main Battle Line[11]	**HKL**	*Hauptkampflinie*
Army Communications	**HNW**	*Heeresnachrichtenwesen*
Army Officers' School	**HOS**	*Heeres-Offizier-Schule*
Army Postmaster	**HPM**	*Heerespostmeister*
HQ	**HQu.**	*Hauptquartier*

11 i.e., the Forward Defended Locality, or Main Line of Battle.

Army Personnel Office	**HPA**	*Heerespersonalamt*
Captain	**Hptm.**	*Hautpmann*
Henschel [aircraft company]	**Hs**	*Henschel-Flugzeugbau*
SS Sergeant-Major	**Hscha.**	*SS-Hauptscharführer*
SS Captain	**Hstuf.**	*SS-Hauptsturmführer*
Army NCOs' School	**HUS**	*Heeresunteroffizierschule*
Army Administration	**HV**	*Heeresverwaltung*
Advanced Dressing Station	**HVP**	*Hauptverbandsplatz*

I

First General Staff Officer (Operations)	**Ia**	*1. Generalstabsoffizier (Führung)*
Second General Staff Officer (Supply and Administration)	**Ib**	*2. Generalstabsoffizier (Versorgung)*
Third General Staff Officer (Intelligence)	**Ic**	*3. Generalstabsoffizier (Feindnachrichtendienst)*
First Adjutant (Officers)	**IIa**	*1. Adjutant (Offiziers-Personalien)*
Second Adjutant (Other Ranks)	**IIb**	*2. Adjutant (Unteroffiziere und Mannschaften)*
Legal Advisor	**III**	*Gericht*
Accounts and Administrative Officer[12]	**IVa**	*Verwaltung*
Doctor	**IVb**	*Arzt*
Divisional Veterinarian	**IVc**	*Veterinär*

12 See also IVz.

Catholic/Protestant Chaplain	**IVd**	*Seelsorge*
Military Economics Officer	**IVWi**	*Wehrwirtschaftoffizier*
Staff Paymaster and Accounting Officer, Field Cashier	**IVz**	
Infantry Gun	**IG**	*Infanteriegeschütz*
in the service of the General Staff	**i.G.**	*im Generalstab(-sdienst)*
Infantry Division	**Inf.Div. (ID)**	*Infanterie-Division*
Infantry	**Inf.**	*Infanterie*
Infantry Regiment	**Inf.Rgt. (IR)**	*Infanterie-Regiment*
Inspector, Inspection	**Insp.**	*Inspektor, Inspektion*
Repair Battalion	**Inst.Btl.**	*Instandsetzungs-Bataillon*
Italian	**ital.**	*italienisch*

J

Fighter-bomber	**Jabo**	*Jagdbomber*
Fighter Commander	**Jafü**	*Jadgfliegerführer*
Jager, Light Infantry	**Jg.**	*Jäger*
Fighter group	**JG**	*Jagdgeschwader*
lit. hunt, or hunting	**Jgd.**	*Jagd*
Jager / Light Infantry Regiment	**JR**	*Jäger Regiment*
Junkers [aircraft company]	**Ju**	*Junkers-Flugzeugbau*
Yugoslavian	**jugosl.**	*jugoslawisch*
Fighter Formation	**JV**	*Jagdverband*

K

Cavalry	**Kav.**	*Kavallerie*
Cavalry Division	**Kav.Div. (KD)**	*Kavallerie-Division*
War Reporters' Company	**KBK(omp.)**	*Kriegsberichter-Kompanie*
Command	**Kdo.**	*Kommando*
Waffen-SS Command	**Kdo.Amt-SS**	*Kommandoamt der Waffen-SS*
Commander	**Kdr.**	*Kommandeur*
Commanding General	**Kdr.Gen. (KG)**	*Kommandierender General*
Commandant	**Kdt.**	*Kommandant*
Command / HQ	**Kdtr.**	*Kommandantur*
Coastal Aviation Group	**K.Fl.Gr. / Kü.Fl.Gr.**	*Küstenfliegergruppe*
Motor Vehicle	**Kfz.**	*Kraftfahrzeug*
Bomber group	**KG**	*Kampfgeschwader*
Prisoners-of-War	**Kgf.**	*Kriegsgefangene*
Battle-group	**Kgr.**	*Kampfgruppe*
Battle-group	**Kpf.Gr.**	*Kampfgruppe*
Lieutenant	**Kptlt.**	*Kapitänleutnant*
Column	**Kol.**	*Kolonne*
Commander of Luftwaffe units attached to an Army High Command	**KoLuft / Koluft**	*Kommandeur der Luftwaffe bei einem Armeeoberkommando*
Corvette	**Korv.**	*Korvette*
Lieutenant-Commander	**Korv.Kpt. (KK)**	*Korvettenkapitän*
Company	**Kp. / Komp.**	*Kompanie*
Tank	**Kpfwg.**	*Kampfwagen*
Corps	**Kps.**	*Korps*

Commander of an Army's Rear Areas	**Korück**	*Kommandeur der rückwärtigen Armeegebiets*
Motorcycle	**Krad**	*Kraftrad (Motorrad)*
Croatian	**kroat.**	*kroatisch*
New intake of Military Medical Officers	**KSON**	*Kriegssanitätsoffizier-nachwuchs*
Courier Squadron	**K.St.**	*Kurierstaffel*
Table of Organisation and Eqpt.	**KStN**	*Kriegstärkenachweisung*
War Diary	**Ktb.**	*Kriegstagebuch*
Coastal Division	**Küst.Div.**	*Küsten-Division*
Coastal Defence Sector	**Küst.Vertg.Abschn.**	*Küsten-Verteidigungs-Abschnitt*
Advanced Corps Section / Det.	**KVA**	*Korps-Vorausabteilung*
War Service Cross	**KVK**	*Kriegsverdienstkreuz*
Motor Vehicle / Tank	**Kw.**	*Kraftwagen / Kampfwagen*
AFV Gun	**Kwk.**	*Kampfwagenkanone*

L

Regional Defence Troops	**Ld.Schtz. / Ldschtz.**	*Landesschützen*
lit. Home Guard	**Ldw.**	*Landwehr*
Legion	**Leg.**	*Legion*
Light	**l.(le) (lei.)**	*leicht*
Latvian	**lett.**	*lettisch*
Light Field Howitzer	**l.F.H.**	*leichte Feldhaubitze*
Air Fleet	**Lfl.**	*Luftflotte*
Training group	**LG**	*Lehrgeschwader*

Air Region[13]	**Lg. / L.G.**	*Luftgau*
Air Region HQ	**Lg.Kdo.**	*Luftgaukommando*
Luftwaffe Inspectorate	**LIn**	*Luftwaffeinspektion*
Aerial Warfare School	**LKS**	*Luftkriegsschule*
Truck / Heavy Goods Vehicle	**LKW / Lkw.**	*Lastkraftwagen*
Airborne Division	**LL.Div.**	*Luftlande-Division*
Aviation Signals	**Ln**	*Luftnachrichten*
Luftwaffe Personnel Office	**LPA**	*Luftwaffen-Personal-Amt*
Glider	**LS**	*Lastensegler*
Senior Medical Officer	**LSO**	*Leitender Sanitätsoffizier*
Leibstandarte-SS "Adolf Hitler"	**LSSAH**	*Leibstandarte-SS "Adolf Hitler"*
Second Lieutenant	**Lt.**	*Leutnant*
Air Defence	**Lv.**	*Luftverteidigung*
Air Defence Command	**Lv.Kdo.**	*Luftverteidigungs-kommando*
Air Force	**Lw.**	*Luftwaffe*

M

Navy	**Mar.**	*Marine*
Messerschmitt [aircraft company]	**Me**	*Messerschmitt-Flugzeugbau*
Medical	**med.**	*medizinisch*
Machine-gun	**MG (Masch.Gew.)**	*Maschinengewehr*
Military	**mil.**	*militärisch*
Military Commander	**Mil.Bef.**	*Militärbefehlshaber*
Major	**Mj.**	*Major*

13 A command and administrative term.

Automatic cannon	**MK**	*Maschinenkanone*
Mobile	**mob.**	*mobil*
Navy High Command	**MOK**	*Marineoberkommando*
Mortar	**Mörs. / Mrs.**	*Mörser*
Motorised	**mot.**	*motorisiert*
Submachine-gun	**Mpi.**	*Maschinenpistole*
Minesweeping	**MS**	*Minensuch-*
Troop Transport	**MTW**	*Mannschaftstransport-wagen*
Munition	**Mun.**	*Munition*
Multi-purpose	**Mz**	*Mehrzweck*

N

Signals Battalion	**Nachr.Abt. (NA)**	*Nachrichten-Abteilung*
Signals Commander	**Nafü**	*Nachrichtenführer*
Short-range Reconnaissance Group	**NAG**	*Nahaufklärungsgruppe*
lit. fog or smoke	**Nbl.**	*Nebel*
Rocket launcher	**Nbl.W.**	*Nebelwerfer*
Dutch	**ndl. / niederl.**	*niederländisch*
Nightfighter group	**NJG**	*Nachtjagdgeschwader*
Signals Officer	**NO**	*Nachrichten-Offizier*
Northern, Northerly	**nordl.**	*nordlich*
Norwegian	**norw. / norweg.**	*norwegisch*
National Socialism	**NS**	*Nationalsozialismus*
Nightfighter Group	**N.Sch.Gr.**	*Nachtschlachtgruppe*
National Socialist Flying Corps	**NSFK**	*Nationalsozialistisches Fliegerkorps*
National Socialist Leadership Officer	**NSFO**	*Nationalsozialistischer Führungsoffizier*

Nightfighter Group	**NSG**	*Nachtschlachtgruppe*
National Socialist Drivers' Corps	**NSKK**	*Nationalsozialistisches Kraftfahrkorps*
National Socialist Welfare Organisation	**NSV**	*Nationalsozialistische Volkswolhfahrt*
Signals Communications	**NVW**	*Nachrichtenverbindungs-wesen*

O

Assistant to Ia[14]	**O1**	*1. Ordonnanzoffizier (bei Ia)*
Assistant to Ib	**O2**	*2. Ordonnanzoffizier (bei Ib)*
Assistant to Ic	**O3**	*3. Ordonnanzoffizier (bei Ic)*
Assistant to Id	**O4**	*4. Ordonnanzoffizier (bei Ia)*
General Assistant and Escort Officer to the Divisional CO	**O5**	*5. Ordonnanzoffizier (Begleitoffizier des Divisionskommandeur)*
Commander-in-Chief	**OB**	*Oberbefehlshaber*
C-in-C of the Army (Air Force) (Navy)	**Ob.d.H. (L) (M)**	*Oberbefehlshaber des Heeres (Luftwaffe) (Marine)*
C-in-C of the Armed Forces	**Ob.d.W.**	*Oberbefehlshaber der Wehrmacht*
SS Brigadier	**Obfhr.**	*SS-Oberführer*
High Command	**Ob.Kdo.**	*Oberkommando*
SS General	**Obstgruf.**	*SS-Oberstgruppenführer*
Senior Field Command	**OFK**	*Oberfeldkommandantur*
Sergeant-Major	**Ofw.**	*Oberfeldwebel*

14 O1-O5 were assistants, and were frequently not appointed ; they were more frequently encountered in late-war SS divisions.

Senior Lance-Corporal	**Ogefr.**	*Obergefreiter*
SS General[15]	**Ogruf.**	*SS-Obergruppenführer*
Army (Air Force) (Navy) High Command	**OKH (L) (M)**	*Oberkommando des Heeres (Luftwaffe) (Marine)*
Armed Forces High Command	**OKW**	*Oberkommando der Wehrmacht*
Lieutenant	**OLt.**	*Oberleutnant*
Aide-de-Camp / Special-tasks Officer	**OO**	*Ordonnanzoffizier*
Operations Section	**Op.Abt.**	*Operationsabteilung*
Senior Quartermaster	**OQ / OQu.**	*Oberquartiermeister*
Aide-de-Camp / Special-tasks Officer	**Ord.Offz.**	*Ordonnanzoffizier*
Organisational Section	**Org.Abt.**	*Organisationsabteilung*
SS Senior Sergeant	**Oscha.**	*SS-Oberscharführer*
Senior Staff Doctor	**OStA**	*Oberstabsarzt*
'Eastern Battalion'	**Ost-Btl.**	*Ost-Bataillon*
SS Lieutenant-Colonel	**Ostubaf.**	*SS-Obersturmbannführer*
SS Lieutenant	**Ostuf.**	*SS-Obersturmführer*
Easterly / Eastern	**ostw.**	*ostwärts*
Organisation Todt[16]	**OT**	*Organisation Todt*
Lieutenant-Colonel	**OtL**	*Oberstleutnant*
Senior Veterinary Surgeon	**OVet**	*Oberveterinär*
Sergeant-Major	**Owm.**	*Oberwachtmeister*
Senior Paymaster	**OZ**	*Oberzahlmeister*

15 Ranking above an SS-Obergruppenführer.
16 Responsible for major civil engineering and construction tasks.

P

Anti-tank Gun	**Pak.**	*Panzerabwehrkanone*
Propaganda Reserve and Training Section	**PEA**	*Propaganda-Ersatz und Ausbildungs-Abteilung*
Panzergrenadier Division / Regt.	**PGD (PGR)**	*Panzergrenadier-Division (-Regiment)*
Engineer	**Pi.**	*Pioniere*
Propaganda Company	**PK**	*Propaganda-Kompanie*
Car	**Pkw (PKW)**	*Personenkraftwagen*
Panzer Training Division	**PLD**	*Panzer-Lehr-Division*
Police	**Pol.**	*Polizei*
Police Division / Regiment	**Pol.Div./Rgt.**	*Polizei-Division/Regiment*
Polish	**poln.**	*polnisch*
Panzer Division	**PD**	*Panzerdivision*
Tank / Armoured...	**Pz.**	*Panzer*
Panzer Battalion	**Pz.Abt.**	*Panzerabteilung*
Panzer Battalion deploying radio-controlled equipment	**Pz.Abt. (Fkl.)**	*Panzer-Abteilung (Funklenk)*
Panzer Army High Command	**Pz.AOK**	*Panzer-Armeeoberkommando*
Panzer Group	**Pz.Gr.**	*Panzergruppe*
Panzergrenadier (Regiment)	**Pz.Gren. (Rgt.)**	*Panzergrenadier (Regiment)*
Tank-hunter / Anti-tank	**Pz.Jg.**	*Panzerjäger*
Panzer Corps	**Pz.K.**	*Panzerkorps*
Panzer Barrier	**Pz.Sperre**	*Panzersperre*
Panzer troops	**Pz.Tr.**	*Panzertruppe*

R

Reich Labour Service	**RAD**	*Reichsarbeitsdienst*
Cyclist (Bicycle Battalion)	**Radf. (Btl.)**	*Radfahrer (Bataillon)*
Minesweeper	**R-Boot**	*Räumboot*
Reichsführer-SS	**Reichsf.SS (RFSS)**	*Reichsführer SS*
Cavalryman	**Reit.**	*Reiter*
Medical Lieutenant	**Rev.Lt.**	*Revier-Leutnant*
Regiment	**Rgt.**	*Regiment*
Captain	**Rittm.**	*Rittmeister*
Knight's Cross	**RK**	*Ritterkreuz*
Air Ministry	**RLM**	*Reichsluftfahrt-Ministerium*
Cavalry Regiment	**RR**	*Reiter-Regiment*
SS Senior Lance-Corporal	**Rttf.**	*SS-Rottenführer*
Rear	**rückw.**	*rückwärtig*
Rumanian	**rum.**	*rumänisch*
Russian	**russ.**	*russisch*

S

Marine Reconnaissance Group	**SA Gr.**	*Seeaufklärergruppe*
Medical (Company / Battalion)	**San. (Kp. / Abt.)**	*Sanitäts (Kompanie / Abteilung)*
Medical Orderly	**Sani**	*Sanitäter*
(Air/Sea) Rescue Area Command	**SBK**	*Seenotbereichskommando*
Motor Torpedo Boat	**S-Boot, S-**	*Schnellboot*
School	**Sch.**	*Schule*

Rapid Brigade	**Schn.Brig.**	*Schnelle Brigade*
Private	**Schtz.**	*Schütze*
Police Force	**Schupo**	*Schutzpolizei*
Heavy	**schw.**	*schwer*
SS Security Service	**SD**	*Sicherheitsdienst (der SS)*
Motor Vehicle for Special Purposes	**Sd.Kfz.**	*Sonder-Kraftfahrzeug*
Independent	**selbst.**	*selbständig*
Heavy Field Howitzer	**s.FH**	*schwere Feldhaubitze*
Self-Propelled	**Sfl.**	*Selbstfahrlafette*
Ground Attack Group	**SG**	*Schlachtgeschwader*
Siebel [aircraft company]	**Si**	*Siebel-Flugzeugbau*
Security Division / Regiment	**Sich.Div. / Rgt.**	*Sicherungs-Division / Regiment*
Heavy Infantry Gun	**s.IG**	*schweres Infanterie-Geschütz*
Security Police	**SIPO**	*Sicherheitspolizei*
Fighter Group	**SKG**	*Schnellkampfgeschwader*
Slovakian	**slow.**	*slowakisch*
Soviet	**sowj.**	*sowjetisch*
Armoured Personnel Carrier	**SPW**	*Schützenpanzerwagen*
SS	**SS**	*Schutzstaffel*
SS Leadership Office	**SS-FHA**	*SS-Führungsamt*
SS troops at the disposal of Hitler or Himmler	**SS-VT**	*SS-Verfügungstruppe*
SS Colonel	**Staf.**	*SS-Standartenführer*
Squadron / Echelon	**Staff.**	*Staffel*
Senior Medical Officer	**St.Arzt. / StA.**	*Stabsarzt*

Staff	**Stb.**	*Stab*
Dive-bomber group	**St.G. / StukaG**	*Sturzkampfgeschwader*
Civilian Administrative Officer (equivalent to a colonel)	**StInt.**	*Stabsintendant*
Garrison Battalion / Company	**St.O.Btl. / Kp.**	*Standort-Bataillon / Kompanie*
SS Lance-Corporal	**Strm.**	*SS-Sturmann*
SS Major	**Stubaf.**	*SS-Sturmbannführer*
Assault Gun[17]	**St.(Stu)Gesch.**	*Sturmgeschütz*
SS Staff Sergeant	**Stuscha.**	*SS-Sturmscharführer*
Dive-bomber	**Stuka**	*Sturzkampfflugzeug*
Veterinary Colonel	**StVt**	*Stabsveterinär*
Southerly / Southern	**südl.**	*südlich*
South-westerly / South-west	**südw.**	*südwestlich*
South-easterly / South-east	**südow.**	*südostwärts*
Searchlight	**Sw.**	*Scheinwerfer*

T

Technical	**techn.**	*technisch*
Part / partially	**teilw.**	*teilweise*
Transport group	**TG**	*Transportgeschwader*
Diary	**Tgb.**	*Tagebuch*
Part-armoured	**t-gep.**	*teilgepanzert*
Part	**Tle.**	*Teile*
Part-motorised	**t-mot. / tmot.**	*teilmotorisiert*
Technical Officer	**TO**	*Technische Offizier*

17 Self-propelled gun.

Pack animal	**Tragt.**	*Tragtier*
Animal Transport Section	**Tragt.Staffel**	*Tragtier-Staffel*
Tropical	**trop.**	*tropisch*
Transport	**Trsp.**	*Transport*
Transport	**Trspw.**	*Transportwesen*
Training Area	**Tr.Üb.Pl.**	*Truppenübungsplatz*
Tunisian	**tunes.**	*tunesisch*
Turkic Battalion	**Turk-Btl.**	*Turk-Bataillon*
Dressing Station	**TVP**	*Truppenverbandsplatz*

U

Junior Doctor	**UArzt.**	*Unterarzt*
Submarine	**U-Boot, U-**	*Unterseeboot*
Corporal	**Uffz.**	*Unteroffizier*
Sub-group	**U.Gr.**	*Untergruppe*
Anti-submarine Vessel	**UJ**	*Unterseeboot-Jäger*
NCO Training Command	**ULK**	*Unterführer-Lehr-Kommando*
Unlimbered	**unbesp.**	*unbespannt*
Hungarian	**ung.**	*ungarisch*
SS Corporal	**Uscha.**	*SS-Unterscharführer*
Research Station	**U-Stelle**	*Untersuchungsstelle*
SS Second Lieutenant	**Ustuf.**	*SS-Untersturmführer*

V

Motor Transport Officer	**V**	*Kraftfahrzeug-Offizier*
Advanced Battalion / Section, Rations Battalion / Section	**VA**	*Vorgeschobene Abteilung, Vorausabteilung / Verpflegungs-Abteilung*
People's Artillery Corps	**VAK**	*Volks-Artillerie-Korps*

Advance Observer	**VB**	*Vorgeschobener Beobachter*
District Defence Command	**VBK**	*Verteidigungs-Bezirks-Kommando*
Liaison	**Verb.**	*Verbindung*
Disposal / Availability (order)	**Verf. / Verfg. / Vfg.**	*Verfügung*
Missing	**verm.**	*vermißt*
supposed / presumed / probably	**vermutl.**	*vermutlich*
Rations	**Verpfl.**	*Verpflegung*
Maintenance	**Vers. / Versorg.**	*Versorgung*
Reinforced	**verst.**	*verstärkt*
Wounded	**Verw.**	*Verwundeter*
People's Grenadier Division	**VGD**	*Volks-Grenadier-Division*
Officer responsible for Ideological Instruction	**VI**	*Weltanschauliche Schulung*
Military Supplies Officer[18]	**VII**	*Militärverwaltung*
Liaison Command for Gliders	**VK (S.)**	*Verbindungskommando für Lastensegler*
Liaison Officer	**VO**	*Verbindungsoffizier*
Outposts	**Vorp.**	*Vorposten*
Outpost Boat	**Vp.**	*Vorpostenboot*
Home Guard	**VS / VST**	*Volkssturm*
Volkswagen	**VW**	*Volkswagen*

18 1939 only.

W

Walloon	**wall.**	*wallonisch*
C-in-C, Armed Forces	**Wbfh. (Wehrm.Bef.)**	*Wehrmachtbefehlshaber*
Military District Command	**WBK**	*Wehrbezirkskommando*
Weather Reconnaissance Squadron	**Wekusta**	*Wettererkundungstaffel*
Mortar	**Werf. / Wf.**	*Werfer*
Westerly, Western	**westl.**	*westlich*
Armed Forces Operational Staff	**WFStab. / WFSt**	*Wehrmachtsführungsstab*
Armed Forces Army (Navy) (Air Force)	**WH (WM) (WL)**	*Wehrmacht Heer (Marine) (Luftwaffe)*
Economics Company[19]	**Wi.Komp.**	*Wirtschaftskompanie*
Military Economics and Equipment Office	**WiRüAmt**	*Wehrwirtschafts-und Rüstungsamt*
Military Region	**WK (Wkr.)**	*Wehrkreis*
Werfer-Lehr-Regiment	**WLR**	*Mortar Training Regiment*
Sergeant	**Wm.**	*Wachtmeister*
Officer of the Guard	**WO**	*Wachoffizier*
Mortar Regiment	**WR**	*Werfer-Regiment*

Z

for example	**z.B.**	*zum Beispiel*
For Special Purposes	**z.b.V.**	*zur besonderen Verwendung*
for a time	**zeitw.**	*zeitweise*

19 Usually found in SS divisions.

Destroyer	**Zerst.**	*Zerstörer*
Platoon	**Zg.**	*Zug*
Twin-engined Fighter Group	**ZG**	*Zerstörer-Geschwader*
Motor Vehicle	**Zgkr. / Zgkw**	*Zugkraftwagen*
Tractor / Prime-mover	**Zgm.**	*Zugmaschine*
Paymaster	**Zm.**	*Zahlmeister*
Naval	**z.S.**	*zur See*
Supply	**Zuf.**	*Zuführung*
together / combined	**zus.**	*zusammen*
available, reserve	**z.V.**	*zur Verfügung*
Munitions / Ordnance Battalion	**z.Btl.**	*Feldzeug-Bataillon*

BIBLIOGRAPHY

Davies, W.J.K. *Wehrmacht Camouflage & Markings 1939–1945. Vehicle Colours, Divisional & Tactical Signs* (London: Almark Publications, 1972)

Dierich, Wolfgang *Die Verbände der Luftwaffe 1935–1945. Gliederungen und Kurzchroniken, eine Dokumentation* (Stuttgart: Motorbuch Verlag, 1976)

Held, Walter *Verbände und Truppen der deutschen Wehrmacht und Waffen-SS im Zweiten Weltkrieg. Eine Bibliographie der deutschsprachigen Nachkriegsliteratur* Bände 1–4 (Osnabrück: Biblio Verlag, 1978–95)

Mehner, Kurt *Die deutsche Wehrmacht 1939–1945* (Norderstedt: Militair-Verlag Klaus D. Patzwall, 1993)

Niehorster, Dr Leo W.G. *German World War II Organisational Series* volumes 3/II & 4/I (N.p.: Privately published, 1992–94)

Oberkommando des Heeres *H.Dv.272* dated 23 May 1943, with changes until the end of the war

Schmitz, Peter & Klaus-Jürgen Thies *Die Truppenkennzeichen der Verbände und Einheiten der deutschen Wehrmacht und Waffen-SS und ihre Einsätze im Zweiten Weltkrieg 1939-1945* Bände 1–4 (Osnabrück: Biblio Verlag, 1987–2000)

Seidler, Franz W. *"Deutscher Volkssturm" – Das Letzte Aufgebot 1944/45* (München/Berlin: F.A. Herbig, 1991)

Tessin, Georg *Verbände und Truppen der deutschen Wehrmacht und Waffen-SS 1939-1945* Band 15 (Osnabrück: Biblio Verlag, 1988)

US War Department *Basic Field Manual FM 30–22: Military Intelligence. Foreign Conventional Signs & Symbols* (Washington, D.C.: US War Dept., July 7, 1942)

US War Department *Technical Manual TM 30–506: German Military Dictionary* (Washington, D.C.: US War Dept., 20 May, 1944)